What people are saying about
RESTORE

"The way that Dana teaches and empowers others is unforgotten. She connects with people, and I know that her readers will be able to feel that through these pages. I cannot wait to see the impact this book will have on the lives of anyone who reads it."

—**GARY KELLER**
Keller Williams Realty International

"Dana is an intentional leader and businesswoman who stewards her intentionality well. She lights up a room and leaves everyone inspired and wanting to think bigger! This is a must-read devotional."

—**JOHN C. MAXWELL**
Leadership Author, Speaker, and Coach

"Dana is a gifted connector and devoted follower of Christ who wants the best for people. Having walked through many challenges herself, I am confident she wrote this ninety-day devotional because she knew you'd be inspired, encouraged, and amazed at how much better your life would become through time with God."

—**LINDA MCKISSACK**
Author of *HOLD*, Podcast Host, RE Investor,
Keller Williams Realty Regional Owner

"From the moment I met Dana, she has inspired and guided me with her leadership and vision. I know this book will touch lives and create the same powerful impact she has had on mine."

—**GABBY MADDOX DAVIS**
Owner/Operator of Keller Williams Atlanta West

"The way that Dana leads and empowers people is unmatched. She connects with people in an unforgettable way, and I know that anyone who reads this book will be able to feel her passion and be impacted each day by its pages."

—**MO ANDERSON**
Oklahoma Hall of Fame, Former CEO of Keller Williams, Author of *A Joy-Filled Life*

"Dana Gentry is one of the most inspiring leaders I know. She leads with wisdom, faith, and excellence—and now she's poured all of that into her new book, *Restore: 90 Days of Intentional Living in Faith, Life, and Business*. I encourage everyone to get this book—it will challenge, encourage, and equip you to live your best life!"

—**DR. DAVE MARTIN**
Speaker, Leader, and Author of *12 Traits of the Great*

"Dana is a rare leader whose intentionality, care for people, and gift for inspiring others set her apart. You'll feel her passion shining through every page and see it come alive in every story. *Restore* invites you to expand your vision and live with purpose as you anchor each day in faith. This is a devotional you'll return to again and again."

—**DIANNA KOKOSZKA**
Speaker, Top 25 Coaches, Author of *Becoming More*

"Dana Gentry is the most intentional business leader that God has placed into my life. She is intentional with the way she leads, the way she speaks, and the way she loves every person within her reach."

—**JAMES TAYLOR DAVIS**
Author of *Parable for the Republic*

"Watching Dana grow into the leader and mentor she is today has been a gift. She leads with purpose, loves with intention, and lifts others with truth. *Restore* embodies her passion for helping others live on purpose and with faith. This book is more than a devotional—it's a blueprint for intentional transformation."

—CHRIS GENTRY
Proud brother, People Leader, Lowe's Companies, Inc.

"Dana is a purposeful and visionary leader whose presence elevates every room she enters. She inspires others to dream bigger, think deeper, and live with greater intention. This devotional is sure to be a powerful and uplifting read."

—JUSTIN ROETHLINGSHOEFER
Founder of OWN IT, Human Health and Performance Expert

"Dana is a leader's leader. She is a connector, and everything that she does brings value to the people around her. I witnessed this when speaking at one of her events, and you can see it in all that she does. I know this book will help many people grow in a deeper way."

—DAMON WEST
Bestselling Author of *The Coffee Bean*

"Having worked with Dana Gentry for several years, she is truly a 1%-er. She stands out above the crowd, she cares for people, and she succeeds in living out her true calling. She is living her passion, and this is just the beginning of her journey leading others to their big life in Christ."

—TERRIE FOSTER-NOWLAND
Executive Business Coach with ICF

RESTORE
90 DAYS OF INTENTIONAL LIVING

Copyright © 2025 by Dana Gentry

Published by AVAIL

All rights reserved. No portion of this book may be reproduced, stored in a retrieval system, or transmitted in any form or by any means—electronic, mechanical, photocopy, recording, scanning, or other—except for brief quotations in critical reviews or articles, without prior written permission of the author.

Unless otherwise specified, all Scripture quotations are taken from the Holy Bible, New International Version®, NIV®. Copyright © 1973, 1978, 1984, 2011 by Biblica, Inc.™ Used by permission of Zondervan. All rights reserved worldwide. www.zondervan.com. The "NIV" and "New International Version" are trademarks registered in the United States Patent and Trademark Office by Biblica, Inc.™ | Scripture quotations marked ESV are from The ESV® Bible (The Holy Bible, English Standard Version®), copyright © 2001 by Crossway, a publishing ministry of Good News Publishers. Used by permission. All rights reserved. | Scripture quotations marked KJV are taken from the King James Version of the Bible. Public domain. | Scripture quotations marked MSG are taken from THE MESSAGE, copyright © 1993, 1994, 1995, 1996, 2000, 2001, 2002 by Eugene H. Peterson. Used by permission of NavPress. All rights reserved. Represented by Tyndale House Publishers, Inc. | Scripture quotations marked NLT are taken from the Holy Bible, New Living Translation, copyright © 1996, 2004, 2015 by Tyndale House Foundation. Used by permission of Tyndale House Publishers, Inc., Carol Stream, Illinois 60188. All rights reserved.

For foreign and subsidiary rights, contact the author.

Cover design by: Todd Petelle
Cover photo by: Andrew van Tilborgh

ISBN: 978-1-969062-04-9   1 2 3 4 5 6 7 8 9 10

Printed in the United States of America

DANA GENTRY

RESTORE
90 DAYS OF INTENTIONAL LIVING

IN

LIFE

FAITH

BUSINESS

Dedication

God, to You be all the glory. I am where I am because of You, the talents I have are on loan from You, and I do what I do every day for You. May my life be a reflection of You in all that I do.

To my husband, Adam: your unwavering support of my dreams, aspirations, big ideas, and goals means more to me than you know, and I am grateful every day for our marriage and partnership. You are one of the most intentional people that I know, and I learn from you every day. Thank you for being my rock and best friend. It's just the beginning of our "big life." I love you.

To my friend and greatest mentor, John C. Maxwell: thank you for teaching me what intentionality truly means eleven years ago, the first time I heard you speak at a conference. You have opened my mind to something new and life-changing. Since that day, you have instilled in me wisdom and hope and have unlocked a mentorship that has shaped the leader and person that I am today. Thank you for being another "father" to Adam and me, and for being so authentically you. I cherish our friendship and love you dearly.

CONTENTS

Acknowledgments . . . . *xvii*
Introduction 21
DAY 1. **A Fresh Start** 24
DAY 2. **Power of Moments** 26
DAY 3. **Winning: Part 1** 28
DAY 4. **Winning: Part 2** 30
DAY 5. **Passion** 32
DAY 6. **Pressure** 34
DAY 7. **Investment Mindset** 36
DAY 8. **Two Types of People** 38
DAY 9. **Missing the Mark** 40
DAY 10. **Contentment** 42
DAY 11. **Perspective** 44
DAY 12. **The Five Ps of Success** 46
DAY 13. **The Four Cs** 48
DAY 14. **Thinking Higher** 50
DAY 15. **Your Uniqueness** 52
DAY 16. **Being a Giver** 55
DAY 17. **Serving** 58
DAY 18. **Your Best Decade Ever** 60
DAY 19. **Thrive in a Downturn** 62
DAY 20. **The Best of the Best** 64
DAY 21. **Happiness** 66

DAY 22.	Leadership Toolkit	68
DAY 23.	The Five Wells of a Morehouse Man	70
DAY 24.	A Reverence	72
DAY 25.	Why Not You?	74
DAY 26.	Seven Intentional Lunch Questions	76
DAY 27.	Personal Definition of Success	79
DAY 28.	Wisdom	81
DAY 29.	Joy	83
DAY 30.	Obedience	85
DAY 31.	Choices	87
DAY 32.	Be a Coffee Bean	89
DAY 33.	Increasing Your Capacity for Stress	91
DAY 34.	Becoming the You of Your Industry	93
DAY 35.	Never Split the Difference: The Power of Negotiation	95
DAY 36.	Becoming Your Future Self	97
DAY 37.	The Six Human Needs: Understanding What Drives You	99
DAY 38.	The Power of Future-Focused Wealth and Health	101
DAY 39.	The Power of Mindset in Life's Unexpected Moments	103
DAY 40.	Reframing Your Mindset with the Story Model	105
DAY 41.	Intentionality as a Success Factor	107
DAY 42.	Your Health	109
DAY 43.	Four Building Blocks of Faith	112
DAY 44.	Leaving a Legacy	114
DAY 45.	Leading vs. Accepting Your Life	116
DAY 46.	Becoming a One Percenter	118
DAY 47.	The Ranch	120
DAY 48.	Childhood Traits	123
DAY 49.	Divine Surprises	126
DAY 50.	Have You Filled a Bucket Today?	128

DAY 51.	The Disease of Distraction	130
DAY 52.	The Good List: Part 1	132
DAY 53.	The Good List: Part 2	134
DAY 54.	The Good List: Part 3	137
DAY 55.	The Law of Intentionality	139
DAY 56.	Motivations	141
DAY 57.	Shake Salt and Shine Light	143
DAY 58.	Extraordinary Leadership	145
DAY 59.	The Secret Sauce: Asking Great Questions	147
DAY 60.	Rooted	150
DAY 61.	Determine to Do the Work	152
DAY 62.	Break Free from a Fixed Mindset	154
DAY 63.	Focus: Part 1	156
DAY 64.	Focus: Part 2	158
DAY 65.	Focus: Part 3	160
DAY 66.	Focus: Part 4	162
DAY 67.	Your Body, His Temple	164
DAY 68.	Obedience Over Performance	166
DAY 69.	Be Where Your Feet Are	168
DAY 70.	Being a Secure Leader	170
DAY 71.	Building	172
DAY 72.	Builders	175
DAY 73.	Whose Job Is It?	177
DAY 74.	Three Leadership Mindsets: Part 1	179
DAY 75.	Three Leadership Mindsets: Part 2	181
DAY 76.	Three Leadership Mindsets: Part 3	183
DAY 77.	Possessing Passion	186
DAY 78.	Deep Work	188
DAY 79.	Vision First, Then Victory	190
DAY 80.	Entrepreneurial Kingdom Work	192

DAY 81. Lessons from Winston Churchill 194
DAY 82. Advice for Younger Generations. 196
DAY 83. The Money Habit of Generosity 198
DAY 84. Lessons from the Great John Wesley 200
DAY 85. Always Exceed Expectations 202
DAY 86. Consistency in Leadership 204
DAY 87. How to *Real* and Not Weird 206
DAY 88. The Three Must-Dos 208
DAY 89. The Four Pictures of God 210
DAY 90. Be a Green Tag Person 213

ACKNOWLEDGMENTS

The journey of writing this book would not have been possible without the countless people who have supported, guided, and believed in me along the way.

To Heather Brockman, my best friend and the world's best implementor. Thank you for "getting me" and for keeping me straight 99 percent of the time. You are intentional with everything that you do, and you are the secret sauce to so much of my intentionality. I would truly be lost without you. Thank you for giving me grace, for always being the first to help me, and for being there for me during all things, big and small. I love you and am so grateful.

To the incredible mentors and coaches I have had along the way, who have shown me what I am capable of and have helped me to live out the calling that God has given me. Thank you, Terrie Foster-Nowland, for coaching me, mentoring me, praying for me, and supporting me in all that I have done for nine years. You are an inspiration to me every day, and you teach and remind me how to live intentionally. Thank you, Larissa Salazar, for walking me through this entire book process, understanding my vision, and then helping it come to life. You are so talented, and I am forever grateful for your coaching and for the impact that Brand Builders Group has had on me.

To Linda McKissack, who has challenged me from day one to think bigger and whose shoulders I have stood on many, many times. Thank you for going first to show me all the things that are possible for me. Without proximity to you, I would not be where I am today. I am so grateful to you for helping me stay intentional for the last decade. I will always speak your name in the rooms I am in, and I value our friendship immensely.

Thank you to my friend, Taylor Davis, who really opened my eyes to two tough questions: "Am I using the talents that God gave me every single day for His glory, and am I putting discipleship at the top of my life bio?" Thank you for writing your great book, *Parable for the Republic*,[1] and encouraging me to truly live out Matthew 25.

Thank you to Dr. Dave Martin for connecting me and Martijn and for being such a great friend and mentor. Without your connection, I would have likely kicked the can down the road a little longer on this book instead of committing and going all in. Thank you to Martijn and the AVAIL team for taking a chance on me, on my first book, and for being so wonderful to work with every step of the way.

To all my Keller Williams family, real estate family, peers, friends, and followers who have supported me in every venture along the way. From the podcast, to Wednesday Morning Mindset days and blogging days, to our wonderful agents in the

---

1 J. Taylor Davis, *Parable for the Republic* (Tulsa, OK: Trilogy Christian Publishing, 2024).

brokerages and in my real estate communities, I am grateful for each of you. We get to choose every day who we show up for, support, and hang around, and I do not take it lightly that you have done that for me. Every day, I pray for those around me, and I am grateful to walk alongside you and lead in the real estate community. It is the place that started it all for me, and it is the place that I love.

INTRODUCTION

FROM DRIFTING TO DEVOTED

On May 8, 2024, I woke up anxious and exhausted. I was having one of those weeks where I was so overwhelmed—so many demands and things that needed my attention or people who needed a decision from me—and I just knew that I needed to pause, or I was going to regret it. I needed to rest and reset. So, I did just that—I canceled all my calls, meetings, and Zooms for the day, packed a journal, pen, water bottle, and chair, and headed to the place that makes me happy, the place where I feel clarity and can think outside in God's creation—the beach.

I plopped down in my chair, taking in the salt air and looking at the beautiful ocean, turned on some worship music, and just started to pray. I loved my businesses and the people I worked with, yet I felt the urge to do something else, to really lean into my passion around growth for businesspeople and leaders, and to refresh those who need refreshing (Proverbs 11:25). I knew that God was calling on me to slow down in order to speed up, to deepen my foundation and share the stories and lessons I have learned in nearly two decades of leadership and business—with zero experience or college degree to lean on.

Writing a book was also always a goal of mine, but I never really knew "why," so I pushed it off. As I was spending time with God this day, listening and being still, it was like an audible voice dropped right into my spirit: *Write your book*. It was clear as day. I listened more, prayed, and tried to be still. I did what any good Christian does. I decided to challenge God (lol) and said, "Okay, God, if you want me to write my book, give me the title." And again, in an almost audible voice, I immediately heard the word **RESTORE**. Loud. Clear. Goosebumps kind of clear. I pulled out my phone and googled the definition for *restore*. Here's what I found:

"Bring back (a previous right, practice, custom, or situation); reinstate. Return to a former condition, place, or position. Repair or renovate."

Then, I googled what the word meant in a biblical context. What does God mean when He says the word *restore*? My search yielded this result:

"To receive back more than has been lost to the point where the final state is greater than the original condition. Making something new again."

Now it all made sense. I immediately thought of all the times throughout my life when God had restored me—over and over again. I felt a sense of peace and gratitude come over me.

The Bible has so much to say about restoration. It's one of God's greatest promises from Scripture. God loves to restore. He restored Job's fortunes (Job 42), Hezekiah's life (Isaiah 38), and David's soul and the joy of his salvation (Psalms 23 and 51).

I began to list all the things that God can restore on the back of an envelope: Your faith, relationships, health, finances, marriage, friendships, spirituality, energy, strength, creativity, business, team, attitude, thoughts, leadership, excitement and joy, brain, life, environment, emotions, and so much more.

It's not easy to be a leader, businessperson, or entrepreneur in today's world. There are many demands, more competition than ever before, many distractions, and overall, less energy and joy in the world for many people. My intention and prayer is that you will treat this book that you are holding as a journal of sorts, carry it around with you for the next ninety days, and lean in so that your life may truly be restored. I pray that you will learn the power of intentionality. If it can take me from a young adult with a panic disorder, no money, and no real direction or guidance in life to the person and leader that I am today, I know that even a little bit of intentionality can catapult you into whatever your heart's next desire is for your life. Thank you for reading and investing in yourself to expand your life and restore yourself to a greater condition than you have ever been!

Be blessed,
Dana

DAY 1
A FRESH START

I believe most people would say that they love a fresh start, making a new year, the first day of a new year to be exact, the perfect time to be intentional about their lives. Intentionality is the one way to get anything you want in life. Every year during the first week of January, my husband, our kids, and I spend a week in Florida with our family, and we create vision boards that showcase intentional things/places/goals that we want to accomplish in that upcoming year. We put them on our phone home screens, print them out, and laminate them to carry around with us. We put them *before us* so that we can focus on being intentional. Whether you picked up this book at the beginning of a year, quarter, month, or a random Tuesday, I believe you are meant to read it and take these next ninety days to read, learn, grow, and practice intentionality in your life, business, and spiritual walk.

I encourage you today—the first day of the next ninety days of your life—to be intentional in a few key areas of your life. Take a moment and *write down* one thing you would like to accomplish in the next three months in each of these categories: spirituality, health, relationships (spouse/kids), business/career, wealth, personal growth, family/friends, adventure/travel, romance, and fun/recreation. This is a great activity to do and share with your family or a team you lead.

Intentionality is the one word I often use to describe the incredible growth I have not only witnessed in my own life, but in the lives of the most successful people I know. Intentional living maximizes your life!

VERSE:

"For we are God's workmanship, created in Christ Jesus for good works, which God prepared beforehand, that we should walk in them."
(Ephesians 2:10, ESV)

DAY 2
POWER OF MOMENTS

Life can be frantic and rushed, and sometimes just feels a little too fast, if I am being honest. We can miss some of life's best moments by moving too quickly, and I have made this mistake many times in my life. I was encouraged by a mentor many years ago to be intentional about taking pictures with my phone of life's most special moments that I would want to remember down the road. I take a LOT of pictures. I know I drive some people crazy with it. Yet, I do it because I want the memories. I want to remember the special moments. The happy, the sad, the powerful, the accomplished, the Spirit-filled, all of them. There is so much for one to learn in the powerful moments of life. If you have ever lost someone or missed a moment in time, you know what it feels like to have the memories of that moment. It is so powerful.

I encourage you today to look back through your phone and "favorite" or categorize a few pictures from last year that were special moments in your life. Make an album for last year's photos, adding the ones that capture your most special moments. Then, think about the lesson you learned from that moment. This is one of my favorite intentional reflection activities to do, and I promise you will be so glad down the road that you did this!

VERSE:

*"[Lord] teach us to number our days,
that we may apply our hearts unto wisdom."*
(Psalm 90:12, KJV)

DAY 3
WINNING: PART 1

Have you ever won anything in life? Maybe it was a sports game, a giveaway, or a big accomplishment at work? Or, maybe, like our cousin Jeff, you have been one of the rare winners of a scratch-off lottery ticket! Wouldn't that be fun?!

There is something about winning that I believe is worth learning.

Here it is: There is absolutely nothing *normal* about winning.

Tim Grover, basketball coach to greats like Kobe Bryant, Michael Jordan, and others, says that "in order to win like the greats do, you must be obsessed." There is a big difference between being interested in something and being obsessed. Interested is a hobby. One of my favorite lessons from Tim is that **interested people manage time, and obsessed people manage focus.** Never forget that, friends.

There are so many distractions today that take us from obsession to only interest. Maybe you started *obsessed*, but after you got some success, you became only *interested* because you got good at it. Or maybe you went from *obsessed* to *interested* for the opposite reason—it started to get a little hard, and you don't like hard things. Either way, to win in today's days and times, you have to be *obsessed*. You have to see this as a good thing, as a passion that God gave you.

I encourage you today, think about the last time you had an unbearable moment or a day when everything went wrong. A time when you told yourself, *I just can't do this anymore*. Remember what you did; don't just feel the emotion. Then, remember that superpower that allowed you to push through. Remind yourself of that today as you think about winning again.

VERSE:

*"Do you not know that in a race all the runners run,
but only one gets the prize?
Run in such a way as to get the prize."*
(1 Corinthians 9:24)

DAY 4
WINNING: PART 2

Yesterday, you read about the difference between being *obsessed* versus *interested*. Today, I want to share three more thoughts with you about winners because I believe everyone has what it takes to be a winner!

Thought #1: Winners require more balance, and remember, you never *find* balance in life; you *create* it. Same with success and happiness. You create them, not find them.

Thought #2: Winners do not let anyone dictate their thoughts and emotions. They don't let something that happened yesterday affect them today. You're carrying someone else's weight with you when you do that. You elevate yourself when "you control you" instead of someone else.

Thought #3: Winners don't win without sacrifice. There is nothing normal about winning at a high level. Everything has a price. The sacrifice to win is so much bigger than everything else.

I encourage you today to look at these three thoughts above and circle or highlight the one you may struggle with the most and would like to shift your mindset on. What action could you take to grow in that area?

VERSE:

"Be wise in the way you act toward outsiders; make the most of every opportunity."
(Colossians 4:5)

DAY 5

PASSION

I think most would agree with me in saying that the most successful and fulfilled people that you know are extremely passionate about what they do.

There are two definitions of the word **PASSION.**

1) Passion (Oxford English Dictionary): a barely controllable emotion.[1]
2) Passion (Latin terminology): "to suffer" (the suffering and death of Jesus).

Excited is different from passionate because you can be excited for something yet unwilling to suffer. You could be excited about an upcoming goal to lose twenty pounds, yet you're not willing to sacrifice your poor eating habits to get to the goal. (That is said with zero judgement, by the way, because I love a good carb myself.) You could be excited about your son or daughter going all in with a sport they love, yet you're not willing to sacrifice your finances, your time, or your own priorities to facilitate their future success.

---

1 Oxford Languages, s.v. "passion," https://www.lexico.com/definition/passion. (Note: Lexico was powered by Oxford and is now archived; the same definition may be found via Google search or the Oxford English Dictionary.)

You must have clarity (the emotion part) and be willing to endure the pain (the suffering part) to be fully passionate. Do you care enough to endure, and not just start? Because starting is the easy part.

How intentional are you with the passion that fills you? How much time are you spending on that passion?

I encourage you today to write down one thing you are most passionate about in your life. It may take a moment to think of something, and if it does, that indicates that you may need some more passion in your life!

VERSE:

"Their hearts are like an oven; they approach him with intrigue. Their passion smolders all night; in the morning it blazes like a flaming fire."
(Hosea 7:6)

DAY 6
PRESSURE

We all face pressure. We all *go through* pressure at some point.

Pressure to perform. Pressure to be the perfect parent or raise the perfect kids. Pressure to act like we've got it all together. Pressure for finances. We all have it because life happens. Sometimes, it is caused by others' decisions that we can't control, and other times, it is caused by our own decisions.

My friend Pastor Daniel Floyd gave such a timely word that I will always remember: *"Pressure will either refine you or confine you. You choose!"*

When pressure confines you, it will shrink you. You shrink back if you don't let it refine you. However, if you let it refine you, God will use the pressure to mold something inside of you that you need. Some areas of your life can only be developed under pressure. The pressure can build faith—if you allow Him to help you.

Remember this: The enemy doesn't have to steal your confidence; he just has to put enough pressure on you. He doesn't have to rob your joy; he just has to put enough pressure on you. This is one of the greatest lessons I've ever learned. *We* give these things up because of the pressure.

What I hope is that you would be intentional about letting that pressure *refine you* when it creeps into your life. We can be intentional with it, or we can let it take us to a place of negativity and scarcity.

I encourage you today to think about any pressure you feel right now, close your eyes, and then give it to God. Give Him the whole situation. Trust that God is with you in this space and is building something inside of you because of it. Not because you are great, but because He is. Trust His faithfulness. He has brought you this far, so He'll be with you now.

VERSE:

"Consider it pure joy, my brothers and sisters, whenever you face trials of many kinds, because you know that the testing of your faith produces perseverance."
(James 1:2-3)

DAY 7
INVESTMENT MINDSET

I believe over the last few years, we, as a population, have fallen victim to an expense mindset. While it is good practice to be aware of your expenses and live fiscally responsible, sometimes I see us departing from the *investment mindset* that we need. I don't necessarily mean financial investments. What I mean is the mindset of investing in people, things, and ways that will come back to you ten-fold in this life.

When you make the time to invest in yourself, you are making the greatest investment of all time. Always bet on yourself, friends, always. When you bet on yourself, it's up to you—and then you can give it back to others.

When you take the time to invest in someone else—like mentor or teach them—you are making an impact. Said another way, this is the parable of reaping what you sow. Investing in yourself and others is sowing good seed. You are feeding yourself with wisdom and guidance that will help you achieve more. Then, when you turn around and pass that on to someone else, you will begin to reap what you have sown.

I encourage you today to think and truthfully answer these questions: Do you have an investment mindset? When is the last time you bet on yourself? When was the last time you said, "Yes, I will choose to spend a couple of hundred or thousand dollars to get into a room where I can invest in others?" If it has been a while, commit to doing it. If you have, maybe it's time you think about the last time you used what you learned to pour into someone else.

VERSE:

*"A man reaps what he sows. . . .
Let us not become weary in doing good,
for at the proper time we will reap a harvest
if we do not give up."*
(Galatians 6:7, 9)

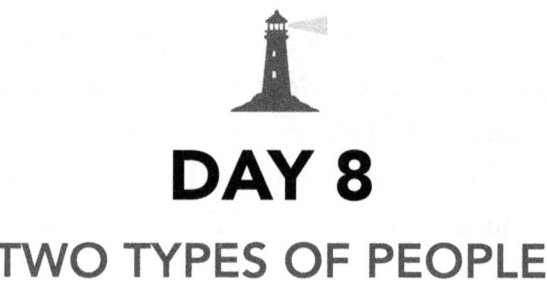

DAY 8
TWO TYPES OF PEOPLE

There are two types of people in this world. There are PEOPLE WHO MAKE THINGS HAPPEN, and there are PEOPLE WHO WAIT FOR THINGS TO HAPPEN. There is quite a big difference.

People who make things happen:

Are grateful and blessed.

Want to grow in every area of their life.

Invest in their health.

Protect their time and their peace.

Know they can do anything they set their minds to.

Hold boundaries and high standards.

Have an "If there's a will, there's a way" attitude.

People who wait for things to happen:

Think things are owed to them or will just miraculously happen.

Think about the life they want but take no action to get it.

Ignore or even harm their health and bodies.

Let life happen to them.

Do not protect or prioritize their time.

Believe they can't do anything.

The good and bad news—whichever way you look at it today—is that you get to choose which type of person you want to be! It is up to YOU!

I encourage you today to examine the characteristics of the people who make things happen. If you focused on it a little more, which one could have the biggest impact on your life right now?

VERSE:

"Now that you know these things, you will be blessed if you DO them."
(John 13:17, emphasis added)

DAY 9
MISSING THE MARK

One of the best quotes I have heard in my lifetime to date is this: *"Doing whatever we want doesn't make us happy; it makes us hollow."*

I love this quote because I have seen this ring true for so many people who truly live without guardrails in their lives. They do whatever they want, and then they wonder why they are not happy or why they are anxious and stressed out. I can remember a time in my life when I was undisciplined. I did not have the guardrails or the accountability that I needed, and I was always left feeling anxious, no matter what I did. It was like something was missing. I had absolutely zero intentionality in my life.

When God created us, He made us to have a relationship with Him. That was the mark. We miss the mark a lot. We disregard the mark when we do whatever we want, whether in our business or our personal lives. Sometimes, what you thought would make you happy makes you feel empty. This is where we need to lean into our relationship with God, and Jesus is not one of many ways to do that; He is the only way. In order not to miss the mark, you may need to evaluate your time and disciplines and decide which areas most need your intentional effort.

I encourage you today to look at your relationship with the Lord and then at your relationship with yourself. Examine the guardrails you have or maybe do not have in your life. Where can you lean in more deeply in your faith and take some accountability for doing "whatever you want to do" all the time? Is there an area you need to focus a little more on—maybe an environment or circumstance you are in, or a bad habit you can't seem to break?

VERSE:

"Therefore, if anyone is in Christ,
the new creation has come:
The old has gone, the new is here!"
(2 Corinthians 5:17)

DAY 10
CONTENTMENT

One thing I have been purposeful about over the last couple of years is walking with the Holy Spirit more because there is a certain contentment that comes with it. Walking with the Holy Spirit gives you more of the YOU that God created you to be. It brings out your spiritual gifts more and more, which is what we are called to do—live in our PASSION and do it all for a MISSION.

As a leader, you should ask yourself these six simple questions to discover your level of contentment and your walk with the Holy Spirit:

1) **Framework:** Who sets the scoreboard for your life? (Are your successes fueled by God or fueled by you?)
2) **Authority:** Who do you submit to? (Living a life submitted to God is the most powerful way to live.)
3) **Time:** Where do you invest your attention? (If you surveyed your weekly schedule, where have you made room for finding your peace?)
4) **Hardship:** What do you lean on when hard times hit? (e.g., alcohol, bad habits, etc.)
5) **Empathy:** Are you growing in compassion for the unlovable? (What do you do when you're offended?)
6) **Relationship:** Are you wholeheartedly following Him?

I encourage you today, take five to ten minutes and quickly jot down your answers to those questions. Journal about them and pray over them.

VERSE:

"And we know that in all things God works for the good for those who love him, who have been called according to his purpose."
(Romans 8:28)

DAY 11
PERSPECTIVE

As I am typing this, I am on an airplane flying to the Dominican Republic with my family to serve on our first mission trip together. I have been on mission trips before, but as a young adult. Not as an "adultier-adult." (Btw, isn't it funny how there is a level of adventure and even fearlessness that we have when we are young, yet as we get older—for me, at least—that diminishes and we can worry about every little thing that could possibly go wrong? Hopefully, it is not just me.) This year, for the first time, I've learned something so profound that has given me a lot of insight into the concept of perspective. The formula is this:

Change of Place + Change of Pace = Change in Perspective

How great is that? Think about it. Have you ever needed a different perspective or to recharge, and just going to the mountains or to the ocean for a weekend and slowing down gave you a whole new outlook? (That is actually how this book came about for me.) That is because you are changing your place (physical environment) and your pace (slowing down, drowning out the noise), resulting in a change in your perspective!

That is exactly what my family is about to embark on over the next six days. We are changing our place and slowing down our pace, and I know a new perspective will come out of this, not to mention our hearts will be forever changed.

I encourage you today to think about the last time you had a change of place and pace. Are you needing a new perspective, and if so, where could you go to slow down even for a day or two, to get a new perspective?

VERSE:

"The eye is the lamp of the body. If your eyes are healthy, your whole body will be full of light."
(Matthew 6:22)

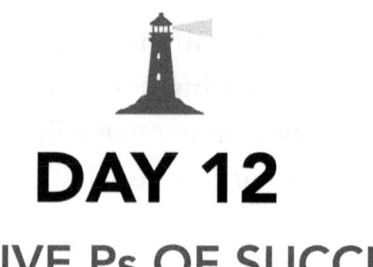

DAY 12
THE FIVE Ps OF SUCCESS

I believe that all leaders—well, all great leaders, at least—are always looking to get BETTER. They want to be wiser, they want to learn more or something new, they want to be challenged so that they can, in turn, lead their people better. Whether they are leading their families, a small group, a foundation, a board, or a company of hundreds or maybe even thousands of employees, they have one thing in common: They want to be better. They want to possess excellence. We will talk about this more later on.

People who want to achieve success need to follow the five Ps:

1) **Be Passionate.** You must possess passion for what you are doing and the mission you are leading. You get God's attention when you give your whole heart to something.
2) **Be Persistent.** Keep going and do not give up. Persistence beats intensity every time. You will find a way if your passion is strong enough. In the Bible, Jesus even tells us that we will "find faith" when we seek.
3) **Be Precise.** Sometimes we aren't winning because we are not being precise enough with what we want. We are not being precise with the actions needed to achieve the results we are looking for.

4) **Be Positive.** Your attitude is the only thing that you get to choose every day. Your attitude matters. It determines who you are, what you do, and what you achieve. Be positive. Have faith. Faith = the confidence in what we hope for and the assurance about what we have not seen (Hebrews 11:1).
5) **Be Praiseful.** Gratitude is the ultimate expression of your faith. Be praiseful during and after the wins. Be praiseful during the hard times and after the hard times. Also, always be praiseful to the people around you whom you appreciate.

Did you know that Jesus cured seventeen bodies, delivered six people from demonic possession, raised three people from the dead, and performed nine miracles over nature (plus many more) just because He lived out these five keys? Wow!

I encourage you today, go through the five Ps and choose the one that you need to work on the most today. Make an effort to go about your day and work on that P. I promise that you will increase in your success when you are intentional about these five things.

VERSE:

"Rejoice in the Lord always. I will say it again: Rejoice! Let your gentleness be evident to all. The Lord is near. Do not be anxious about anything, but in every situation, by prayer and petition, with thanksgiving, present your requests to God. And the peace of God, which transcends all understanding, will guard your hearts and your minds in Christ Jesus."
(Philippians 4:4-6)

DAY 13
THE FOUR Cs

Years ago, I learned one of the most powerful models that I have since implemented: the Four Cs Model, which was created by Strategic Coaching and is now widely used across the world. Once you learn this model, you can't "unlearn it." It sticks. And it proves to be true for nearly every successful or significant thing you accomplish in life.

> "The 4 C's Formula is a universal process that can be used by anyone who wants to achieve greater success in any part of their life."[2]
> —Dan Sullivan

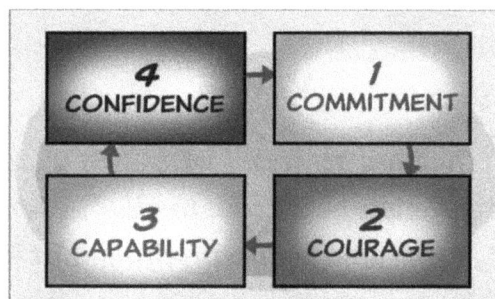

It starts with **commitment.** Most people think that you need all the other Cs first before you start—capabilities, courage, and

---

2 Dan Sullivan, *The 4 C's Formula: Your Building Blocks of Growth: Commitment, Courage, Capability, and Confidence* (Ethos Collective, 2021).

confidence. But you don't need any of those things before you make a big commitment. You gain the rest after you commit. That's what makes this model work so well.

Think about it. Anytime you have succeeded at something, you first made a big, intentional commitment. It was probably scary; it probably made you want to throw up or wet your pants, but you committed. For me, a great example is writing this book! I am no author by trade. I have absolutely no writing capabilities, nor did I even have the courage to do this. I had to pay the money, pick the publisher, and just COMMIT. Then, I began to research, write, get more courage, and gain the capabilities and confidence, but they all came second to my commitment. When faced with fear, you have two choices: You can avoid it, or you can have the courage to push through. Commitment opens up possibilities; it allows breakthroughs to happen, and it creates the courage to push through.

I encourage you today to ask yourself, *When was the last time I made a big commitment?* Nine out of ten times, the burnout and boredom businesspeople and leaders often feel happens because they need to make a new, big commitment to get their butts out of complacency and into significance again. Where do you need to commit today?

VERSE:

"You and these people who come to you will only wear yourselves out. The work is too heavy for you; you cannot handle it alone."
(Exodus 18:18)

DAY 14
THINKING HIGHER

Have you ever felt stuck in your leadership, and you could not think more broadly or grow more because you were stuck in the mud? Many mentors have encouraged me to get to the 30,000-foot view instead of the 100-foot view because you can stay in the weeds and not think big enough. I have found throughout the years that I am sometimes too close to the situation or the people involved.

As a leader, you have to create emotional distance at times. You can lose objectivity in identifying the right thing to do when you care and love so much, and eventually, you lose credibility with those you lead if you do not do something about it.

If you find yourself in this situation, ask yourself, *What problem am I really trying to solve?* Don't just address the symptoms of the problem, but get to the actual root. This will help you think higher and create emotional altitude. If you find yourself in a really difficult situation, ask these questions:

1) If a great leader replaced me today, what would they do?
2) If no one's feelings got hurt, what would I do?
3) If I were advising someone else on their business and this situation, what would I coach them to do?

All these questions help create emotional distance . . . and allow you to be objective.

Remember, if you are too close to any situation, you are losing effectiveness!!! Always. Force yourself to create objectives.

I encourage you today to think about whether you may be too close to a situation. Write it down. Then, ask those three questions truthfully and journal your responses.

VERSE:

"What do you know that we do not know?
What insights do you have that we do not have?"
(Job 15:9)

DAY 15
YOUR UNIQUENESS

I have had the pleasure of learning from one of the, if not THE, best branding experts in the world, Rory Vaden with Brand Builders. Rory has taught me an incredible amount about marketing and branding, so much so that I hired his team to help with the launch of this book and the brand! I was hooked the first time I heard Rory speak about finding your uniqueness. This intrigued me. These big-name leaders/speakers can all be described with one word that makes them unique.

Let me give you a few examples:

1) Dave Ramsey . . . Debt
2) Brené Brown . . . Shame
3) Tony Robbins . . . Pain
4) Mother Theresa . . . Poverty
5) Martin Luther King, Jr. . . . . Inequality

We could go on and on. Yet, when I discovered the formula for finding and narrowing down what makes me unique, everything changed for me and my brand/business. You can find yours too, and here's how:

Ask yourself the questions:

1) What problem do I solve?
2) What am I passionate about?
3) What is the problem and cause?

Rory Vaden shares such an impactful way to think about this. He says, *"You are powerfully positioned to serve the person you once were."*[3]

So think about it, who did you used to be? What was your problem? What caused it? And how could you help someone now overcome that same problem? THAT is your uniqueness.

I was a successful yet drifting woman. I had no real vision for my life, let alone a plan. I had no accountability. I wasn't in the right environments or rooms. I wasn't super educated. (I am a college dropout.) I had battled horrible panic attacks and had unhealthy habits. Yet, I did have my faith, a strong work ethic, great people skills and emotional intelligence, energy and drive, creativity, and the desire to do something bigger, something more. All of that changed when I got intentional with my life. Intentional with my peers, my habits, my health, my mentors and coaches, my learning and education, my relationships, etc. I became intentional in everything, and because of that, my life grew exponentially! My problem was stagnation, and my uniqueness is intentionality.

---

[3] Rory Vaden, "How to Find Your Brand's Uniqueness," blog post, RoryVaden.com, accessed August 7, 2025, https://roryvaden.com/blog/personal-branding/how-to-find-your-brands-uniqueness/.

I encourage you today to take a moment and work through the questions above. Jot down who you used to be. Work through the questions and start the process of thinking about what your uniqueness could be!

VERSE:

"And even the very number of hairs on your head are numbered. So don't be afraid; you are worth more than sparrows!"
(Matthew 10:30-31)

DAY 16
BEING A GIVER

We will discuss giving multiple days in this book. Why? Because at their core, every human was designed to give and serve. The most successful people I know are givers. They don't care about what they get back; they give out of pure joy and because they have a giver's heart. I have always said that I want others to describe my legacy as "the most generous person I know!" That is a tall task when you are friends with great givers like my friends Linda McKissack, Mo Anderson, John Maxwell, Heather Brockman, and many, many others!

I am blessed with great givers around me. You can think of some, too, I am sure. The first to raise their hand and give when something is needed, the first to step up and say, "I can help!" the first to donate or show up with a gift when they don't need to. I want to be so outrageously generous that it shocks people! I want to always give more than I take. I want to live a life where I am encouraging more people to stand up and be givers in an intentional way. Why? Because if you are breathing, you need encouragement and help in some area of your life. It is rare that I ever show up without a gift for someone I meet, see, or spend time with. It could be as little as an impactful book I just read, a little trinket that made me think of them, or something I saw that I just knew they would like. It is not about the actual material possession; it is about the genuine desire to make them smile and be generous to them. People ask me frequently how I make time for this. Simple. I am intentional about it. I keep a note in my app on my iPhone titled "gift ideas," and every time I hear someone mention something they like or would like to do, I add it to the note. Intentionality around being a genuine giver can lead to such great relationships and open doors.

I know what you are thinking, and it is not always about the money. Some people think the only way to give is with money, and that is not the case. One of the most impactful books I have read in my life is a book called *Chase the Lion* by Mark Batterson. It's one of my top three favorite books of all time. In the book, Batterson talks about the three things you should focus on and be intentional about with your giving. Those three things are your time, your talents, and your treasures. You can give your time, you can give of your talents (your gifts that only you possess), and you can give treasures (money or things). The key takeaway is that if you don't take action, nothing changes in your giving.

I encourage you today to think about who you could wow with a simple gift of giving. When was the last time that you actually gave a gift to someone special to you? Do you need to start a simple note in your phone to be more intentional?

VERSE:

"Each of you should give what you have decided in your heart to give, not reluctantly or under compulsion, for God loves a cheerful giver."
(2 Corinthians 9:7)

DAY 17
SERVING

I believe most leaders can say that they want three things: *purpose, peace, and profit.*

Business owners, leaders, or entrepreneurs have difficult days, and there are times they may ask themselves, *Why am I even doing this?* It is usually peace they are seeking. I am going to clue you in on a secret today to help with that, and the secret is this . . . *the path to peace is service!* Intentionally serving. Serving others should be at the core of why you do what you do as an effective leader.

There are self-centered leaders and there are service-centered leaders in this world. Serving others is your superpower to success and peace when you are leading. When you are serving others, there are only WINS!

There is no fear when the mission is clear. As a leader, your mission is to serve your people.

You see it in the greatest leaders out there. They serve their people well. The best business owners show up and serve their people well. The best doctors, lawyers, realtors, financial advisors, teachers, board members, foundation founders, etc. If you are looking for more peace as a leader, you may need to adjust your mindset and start serving a little more.

I encourage you today to think about who you can serve that would make a big difference in their life or role. Who comes to mind? Ask yourself, *Have I spent intentional time serving those I lead in the last month or so?* If not, that is okay. Today is a great day to start!

VERSE:

"For even the Son of Man did not come to be served, but to serve."
(Mark 10:45)

DAY 18
YOUR BEST DECADE EVER

Dan Sullivan, founder of Strategic Coaching, did an exercise about living your best decade ever, which really means, what do you want the next ten years of your life to look like? You begin by identifying your age ten years from now. Think about that for a moment. Ten years from today, what year will it be? How old will you be?

There are three key categories you should focus on to have your next best decade ever. Those are:

1) Creativity/Productivity
2) Fitness/Health
3) Family

You can ask yourself certain questions about each category to stir your brain on what the next decade needs to look like to be the best. In the creativity and productivity space, what needs to be true for the next ten years to be the best in your business/production space? Who are the "whos" that you need in order to make that happen? What does time look like for you? Do you need to speed things up to make it happen, or are you ready to start slowing down?

In the fitness and health space, what would be the hardest thing for you to do if you were ten years older? What top three things do you want to accomplish in the fitness and health space over the next ten years? What do you need to learn more about?

What top three things do you want to accomplish in the family space? How can you let these goals PULL YOU more towards your future self instead of you pushing yourself there?

Dan Sullivan always says that your business and the people you work with should be easy, lucrative, and fun. If you can ensure that happens and define the top three achievements that would make your next decade the best one ever in each category above, then you can live a life of success.

I encourage you today to spend the next five to fifteen minutes thinking about your next ten years. Looking at the above categories, what are the top three things in each one that you would like to accomplish to make this your best decade ever? Write them down. Save them somewhere where you will review them more often each year.

VERSE:

*"This is what the LORD says—your Redeemer,
the Holy One of Israel: 'I am the LORD your God,
who teaches you what is best for you,
who directs you in the way you should go.'"*
(Isaiah 48:17)

DAY 19
THRIVE IN A DOWNTURN

No matter what line of business, work, or ministry you are in, we all have seasons of downturns. It could be the market or the economy that causes the downturn, or it could be something as wild as a total worldwide pandemic like we had in 2020. No matter the reason, there are always things that you can do to pull yourself out of the slump and begin to thrive again!

1) **Start with MINDSET.** Be resourceful and realistic about the downturn. Be the most knowledgeable person in your field.
2) **Focus on your RELATIONSHIPS.** Work on what you learned yesterday. Prioritize reciprocity and become the person others look to for guidance because of your reputation for helping. Bring people value. Help them understand things better. Deepen and develop your key relationships.
3) **Take ACTION.** This may be my favorite one. You may have heard one of my favorite quotes, "Activity breeds activity!" and it is so true. Just do something. Get to trainings, motivational seminars, masterminds, and other events. Expand what you are learning. Get back to the basics. Do what has always worked. Work on your growth plan for yourself.

Focus on these two quotes to thrive in a downturn:

- *"Your eyes can only find what your brain is looking for."*[4]
  —Dan Sullivan
- *"Opportunity is never lost, it is always found by someone else."*
  —a common quote from Dianna Kokoszka

I encourage you today to think about what you need to do if you are in a downturn or not seeing the results you would like. Think about the three things above. How is your mindset? How are your key relationships? Are you taking action? If not, what can you do today to change?

VERSE:

"May the LORD, the God of your ancestors, increase you a thousand times and bless you as he has promised!"
(Deuteronomy 1:11)

---

[4] Dan Sullivan, statement on Strategic Coach website, accessed August 7, 2025, Strategic Coach, "Dan Sullivan" profile page, https://www.strategiccoach.com/coach/dan-sullivan.

DAY 20
THE BEST OF THE BEST

I love to hear a great story; they inspire and encourage me so much. I once had the privilege of hearing the story of how Michael Jordan hired Tim Grover as his coach who ultimately led M. J. to be the best basketball player of all time. The story goes like this.

Tim Grover had just begun his coaching career and knew he needed more athletes to coach. He wrote letters to players about his experience and how he could coach them to their next level of success. One day, he wrote letters and mailed them to several players on the Chicago Bulls, hoping he would get a call from at least one of them. He did not mail a letter to Michael Jordan because he already had a great coach, and he was untouchable. A few months later, Tim Grover got a phone call from someone who worked with Michael, saying that M. J. had requested a meeting with Tim to discuss the coaching opportunities that he had presented in his letter. Tim was shocked because he knew that he had not mailed any of his letters to M. J. Turns out, M. J. had overheard the other players talking about the letters they had received. Those players did not seem interested in hiring another coach; so, for whatever reason, they did not take action. But M. J. wanted to know more. This led to a meeting, which led to years of an incredible relationship between M. J. and Tim Grover and much success for both—playing and coaching.

When Tim Grover was asked why he thought M. J. reached out when no one else had—especially since he never even sent M. J. a letter—Tim's response was so powerful. (I will never forget the moment I heard him say this at an event in Austin, Texas.)

His answer: "Because **the best of the best are ALWAYS looking to get better.**"

Wow. So powerful. And so true.

The best of the best, in anything, are *always, always* looking to get better! They are learning-oriented.

How great is that?

I think we could all agree, M. J. was definitely the best of the best in basketball.

I encourage you today to think about this: What do you want to be the best at? What are you already the best at? How are you getting better and better? Remember, if you are a Christian, you are called to excellence in all you do. You should want to be the best, not for selfish reasons, but because you are working for the Lord.

VERSE:

"Whatever you do, do all to the glory of God."
(1 Corinthians 10:31, NIV)

DAY 21
HAPPINESS

Happiness is a fun thing to talk about for most people but sometimes harder for other people. There are many reasons why someone could be happy or unhappy in their life. Yet, I do believe that 99 percent of the time, it is a choice. It starts with controlling your mind and protecting your thoughts, which Jesus tells us in the verse below.

If you let other people control your thoughts and emotions, chances are, you are not in control of your happiness.

I once heard my mentor, Gary Keller, say, *"If you took away everything I have, but I still had my faith, health, and relationships, I would be better than most."* This struck me so profoundly because first, Gary is a billionaire, so he knows what it is like to be blessed with more than most. Secondly, what he said is, to me, the definition of happiness: If you have your faith, you can be happy no matter the circumstance you may face because you know the Lord is in control.

Happiness is much like success in my mind; you don't *find it*, you **create it**. Those are two very different things.

Also, where there is a winner or a successful person, there is balance. Balance operates the same way as happiness: You don't find it. You create it. This is encouraging because you can create your way to happiness, no matter the situation.

I encourage you today to think about where you find your happiness. Where does it come from? Do you need a pep in your step for your happiness today? Or do you have happiness overflowing from you, and if so, who can you help and encourage today with your happiness?

VERSE:

"Finally, brothers and sisters, whatever is true, whatever is noble, whatever is right, whatever is pure, whatever is lovely, whatever is admirable—if anything is excellent or praiseworthy—think about such things."
(Philippians 4:8)

DAY 22
LEADERSHIP TOOLKIT

I once heard Chick-fil-A describe themselves as a "leadership development company disguised as a fast-food place," and I absolutely loved this thought. They are still one of the only companies whose college employees are ranked higher in the acceptance process because of their experience working there. That is incredible. I learned about this valuable "leadership toolkit" from Dan Cathy, son of Truitt Cathy, who founded Chick-fil-A, and I believe all leaders will find it valuable. My hope is that you may even order the items listed below from Amazon, Walmart, or other stores as visuals to demonstrate important leadership lessons with the people you lead. I hear so often that leaders want to intentionally grow the people they serve, yet they struggle knowing how to. This is such a great and meaningful example that could impact your people for years to come.

Leadership Toolkit Objects:

1) **A Shoe Shining Brush:** Because all great leaders serve others. They are always looking for ways to serve.
2) **Oxygen Mask:** Because just like they say, "Put your mask on first" on an airplane, you should learn and lead the way for

your folks to follow, and you should be able to help them. You cannot fill from an empty cup.

3) **A Metal Baton:** Because success is about handing off the baton, known as "succession." When you drop the baton on concrete or a hard floor, the sound is very loud and horrible, yet that is what happens when you, the leader, try to pass the baton to the wrong person or in the wrong way. It is a huge piece of leadership.

4) **A Slinky:** There are three very powerful lessons you can learn from a slinky.
   > *Leaders have to lead.* You have to be clear. You are the front line that starts it all. Everything rises and falls with leadership.
   > *Leaders develop followers.* Others love to follow a great leader; it's what makes everything get into motion when you keep creating great followers and other leaders.
   > *Followers become the next generation of leaders.* This is the slinky flipping end over end over and over again, which represents bringing and moving new leaders up.

I encourage you today: If you are a leader, get your toolkit together and start using visuals to become a better leader and help the people you are leading understand as well.

VERSE:

*"May his days be few;
may another take his place of leadership."*
(Psalm 109:8)

DAY 23

THE FIVE WELLS OF A MOREHOUSE MAN

Dr. Robert Franklin, the tenth Morehouse President, popularized the five expectations of leadership for Morehouse Renaissance Men, and are incredible ways to remember things that will serve you well into your leadership journey and career. These values are the foundation of the Morehouse 1867 philosophy of living beyond the halls of academia, and they still ring true today.

THE FIVE WELLS OF A MOREHOUSE MAN
(In this specific order):

1) Well-read
2) Well-spoken
3) Well-dressed
4) Well-traveled
5) Well-balanced

I'd like to expand on well-spoken and well-traveled. Well-spoken means not opening your mouth before you know something. You do not speak just to speak, especially when it could be false.

Well-traveled is a huge one because it is important to become cultured, understand the world around you, and seek out your competition. Go travel to the most exciting business spaces today and see what's happening.

I encourage you today to write the Five Wells down somewhere where you can see them frequently and meditate on them. Which one jumps out at you the most that you need to work on?

VERSE:

"From the fruit of their lips people are filled with good things, and the work of their hands brings them reward."
(Proverbs 12:14)

DAY 24
A REVERENCE

I want to start today with a question: Do you have reverence for the work that you do every day?

One definition of reverence is *"to have honor or respect that is felt or shown; to regard or treat with respect."*[5]

Do you really love and respect the work that you do?

Pioneers break ground; they never build the greatest, but they inspire other people to build the greatest because of their love and respect for what they do. They study examples of excellence and places that inspire them; they are intentional about spending time with people who are already living out their dream. These are all ways that they become more and more reverent for the work they do day in and day out. It starts with the vision first, not the skill—and eventually, you'll grow in reverence for the vision. Some of the best leaders that I have had the privilege of learning from, like Gary Keller, are intentional daily about bringing value to those around them through their tremendous reverence for the people they come in contact with. Gary studies the profession

---
[5] Merriam-Webster, s.v. "reverence," *Merriam-Webster.com Dictionary*, https://www.merriam-webster.com/dictionary/reverence.

every single day, when, quite frankly, he does not need to. Yet, he continues to study because of his great reverence for his life's work. I respect him tremendously for this.

I encourage you today to be honest with yourself and think about the word *reverence*. Do you have it right now in the work you do each day? Whether it's taking care of your family and kids, leading a big company, working for a foundation, volunteering, or running your small business, do you respect and love your work? If the answer is no, then reread the above and journal about your vision and what you may need to change or explore more deeply to seek the reverence that you need.

VERSE:

"Whatever you do, work at it with all your heart, as working for the Lord, not for human masters."
(Colossians 3:23)

DAY 25
WHY NOT YOU?

One question I love to ask myself and the leaders I coach is, *"Why not you?"*

Somebody is going to do what you want to do. In fact, someone likely already has—many people likely have!

So, why not you?

What big things are important to you? What would you do if you knew you wouldn't fail? What would you do if money were not an issue or an objection? What would you do if you thought it would be easier? If you can imagine it, then someone has already done it. Just reading that should calm your nervous system and encourage you that it is possible!

Doing hard things actually strengthens you. So do hard things!

Invest in yourself—into your skillset, your relationships, etc. When you do that, anything is possible.

I encourage you today to think about the one thing you would like to do that fear has been holding you back from. Name it. Write down your thoughts on why you think you can't do it. Then, write down why you CAN do it. What would hold you back?

VERSE:

"Jesus looked at them and said,
'With man this is impossible,
but with God all things are possible.'"
(Matthew 19:26)

DAY 26
SEVEN INTENTIONAL LUNCH QUESTIONS

One of the most powerful and impactful lessons that I have learned from my mentor, John Maxwell, is the model for an intentional mentor lunch session, and that's what I want to share with you today. Every month, you should have at least one lunch with someone bigger and better than you so that you can learn, grow, get great experience, and learn to ask important people great questions!

Ask these seven questions:

1) What is the greatest lesson you have ever learned?
2) What are you learning right now?
3) How has failure shaped your life?
4) Who do you know that I should know?
5) What have you read that I should read?
6) What have you done that I should do?
7) How can I add value to you?

I want to share with you a story about my brother, Chris Gentry, and how these questions have impacted his life. He attended our "I Love Coaching Whole Life Summit" in 2023 and heard John speak about these seven questions. John encouraged the attendees to invite someone they could learn from and develop a relationship with to lunch within thirty days. My brother has been employed at Lowe's, the home improvement store, since he was eighteen years old. He has climbed the ladder of success and been recognized as one of the youngest leaders to get promoted with each promotion he has received. He thought it would be a shot in the dark, but the next day, after hearing John speak, he decided to email the president and CEO of Lowe's, Marvin Ellison, and ask for a mentor lunch.

Truthfully, he wasn't sure he would even get a response, considering there are over 300,000 employees in the company. He knew that Marvin loved John Maxwell, so he mentioned that if he had time to meet, he had one of John's books he'd like to give him. To his surprise, within forty-eight hours, Marvin responded, saying he would love to meet and that his assistant would be in touch. Chris was excited yet wanted to contain it because he wasn't sure whether the assistant would actually reach out. Within twenty-four hours, she did, and the meeting was set! Chris traveled to Charlotte, North Carolina, for his mentor lunch with Ellison, gave him John's book, and asked questions. The lunch was so impactful and career-changing for Chris. The time with Marvin was invaluable. The lesson from John . . . even more invaluable.

Chris and John Maxwell Chris and Marvin Ellison

I encourage you today to meditate on the lesson here, which is to take action on what you learn! Don't be afraid to ask. Have great questions.

VERSE:

"Remember your leaders, who spoke the word of God to you. Consider the outcome of their way of life and imitate their faith."
(Hebrews 13:7)

DAY 27
PERSONAL DEFINITION OF SUCCESS

As a leader, you need a personal definition of success. You have to find yourself before you can improve yourself. Here is how you do that:

1) You have to know your purpose in life.
2) You have to know what you are passionate about.
3) You have to know your natural abilities. What are you good at?

We are wired to do what we are passionate about. Passion gives you energy!! This is usually your giftedness, the strengths that God gave you for success. I like to say this:

Success = Passions + Strengths

If you are good, you can have any brand or any marketing. A lot of us just need to focus on getting good!

I encourage you today to answer the three questions above as best you can and to go with whatever comes to mind first. You will be well on your way to defining your personal definition of success.

VERSE:

"Each of you should use whatever gift you have received to serve others, as faithful stewards of God's grace in its various forms."
(1 Peter 4:10)

DAY 28
WISDOM

I started this book sharing a little about the importance of wisdom and would like to go deeper today because I believe it is one of the most important things for you to glean from this book in order to become more intentional in your life, business, and faith.

My friend, Dr. Dave Martin, who is one of the wisest people I know, shares that wisdom is his favorite topic to speak on, and here is why.

The only problem you will really ever have is a wisdom problem. It's because you don't know what you don't know. If your marriage is struggling, you don't have a marriage problem; you have a wisdom problem because you need to learn more about the biblical principles of a great marriage. If you have a money problem, you have a wisdom problem because you need to learn more about the biblical principles of money. The list goes on and on.

We must be intentional about learning and growing in wisdom every day. The Bible teaches us that in Proverbs 1. Wisdom gives us a divine advantage in life! I was so passionate about writing this ninety-day devotion because I understood this, and when I did, it changed my life. I want to help you change yours too.

I encourage you today to ask yourself, *In what area of my life do I need more wisdom?* Money? Relationships? Business? Leadership? Parenting? Health? Pray today for God to give you wisdom in those areas, and then search the Bible for more wisdom on those topics and study them.

VERSE:

"Let the wise listen and add to their learning, and let the discerning get guidance."
(Proverbs 1:5)

DAY 29

JOY

I am going to go out on a limb here and say that a lot of people out there in the world today need to work on getting their JOY back. Many people need to understand that when you get your joy back, you actually get your strength back too! When I look back on my life, I realize there were plenty of times when my joy was not there. What I did during those times—and how intentional I was about getting my joy back—was the key. If I am being honest, it wasn't always easy.

I had to fight internally to focus on it.

Burnout is common for leaders, business owners and businesspeople, entrepreneurs, and people in ministry. I have found that when we focus on being joyful, a lot of things automatically fall into place.

Joy isn't out there somewhere; it is right here! It's easy to focus on thinking that joy is only out there for some people, or that it's unattainable for you in this season. However, joy is a choice, and sometimes we lose sight of everything we have right now that can and does bring us joy. Joy should pop out of you, especially as a person of faith. Joy is to be released, not reserved. Don't save it for later. The season is now.

I encourage you today to think about and write down what truly brings you joy. When was the last time you felt overjoyed? What do you need to do to be more intentional about getting more joy in your life?

VERSE:

"Do not grieve, for the joy of the LORD is your strength."
(Nehemiah 8:10)

DAY 30
OBEDIENCE

Today, I want to start a little differently. Drop down and read the verse of the day FIRST.

Now, I want you to circle or highlight the word "IF"—that's the keyword here.

Obedience is a choice. An intentional choice. You are either obedient or not obedient. This plays out in your health, in your wealth, in your business, in your relationships, and in your faith and relationship with Jesus—obedience is important in every single aspect of your life. God rewards obedience! God blesses obedience, pure and simple. This doesn't mean you have to be perfect. Nobody is perfect, not even the people God blessed in the Bible. But they did obey God more often than not in most areas of their lives. Promotion always follows obedience.

I encourage you today to just start walking in obedience and see if the hand of God and His blessings aren't magnified and multiplied in your life. In what area of your life do you need to practice more intentional obedience? Your health? Your money? Your faith? Your relationships?

VERSE:

*"If you are willing and obedient,
you will eat the best from the land."*
(Isaiah 1:19)

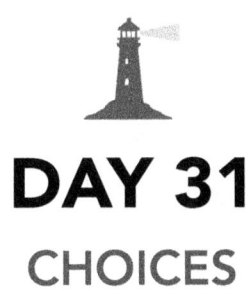

DAY 31
CHOICES

One of the best things I have learned in my business career over the last two decades is this: *You're either preparing yourself for the next opportunity or robbing yourself of it based on the decisions you make.*

These are such great words of wisdom, especially for anyone who is an achiever, a leader, or generally looking to grow. From this quote, you should ask yourself, *Am I making the right decisions on the right activities every day? Do I slack on generating leads for more business when I shouldn't? Do I run a profit-first business and cut expenses when needed? Do I have difficult conversations and move people out of roles that are not the right fit for them? Or do I coast through life—or drift, rather—and are my poor decisions ultimately costing me my next opportunity?*

I meet a lot of leaders who are looking for their next opportunity and searching for more, yet they are not making the right daily decisions to set themselves up for that next opportunity. They wonder why they aren't getting chosen or called on next, or maybe even why they aren't seeing the results that they want, yet they won't look more deeply into what they need to do and then do it.

I encourage you today to think about any decisions that you haven't been making but should be. Is there anything you know deep down that you should be doing to prepare for your next opportunity? Do you feel prepared for it? What work do you need to do to prepare?

VERSE:

"But if serving the LORD seems undesirable to you, then choose for yourselves this day whom you will serve . . . But as for me and my house, we will serve the LORD."
(Joshua 24:15)

DAY 32
BE A COFFEE BEAN

Damon West had everything—an education, a great job, and a promising future. But addiction took hold, and within eighteen months, he went from working on Wall Street to being homeless and committing crimes to fund his drug habit. Arrested and sentenced to sixty-five years in a Texas maximum-security prison, he faced what most people fear the most—prison life.

He was told that prison would either make him a **carrot** (soft and weak when boiled), an **egg** (hard and bitter when boiled), or a **coffee bean**—someone who changes the environment around them for the better. Inspired by an older inmate named Mr. Jackson, Damon intentionally chose to be a coffee bean. This ONE ACT of intentionality completely changed his life. He rejected gangs, stayed positive, and transformed not only his own life but also the lives of those around him. Seven years later, he was miraculously granted parole. Today, he is a professor, a worldwide speaker, and an author, sharing his message of hope and transformation worldwide.

Life is like a pot of boiling water. Challenges and adversity will come. You have a choice—let them break you (like the carrot), harden you (like the egg), or transform you into something better (like the coffee bean).

I encourage you today to think about a difficult situation in your life. How have you been reacting—like a carrot, an egg, or a coffee bean? Make an intentional choice today to transform your environment rather than letting it change you.

VERSE:

"Whoever walks with the wise becomes wise, but the companion of fools will suffer harm."
(Proverbs 13:20, author paraphrase)

DAY 33

INCREASING YOUR CAPACITY FOR STRESS

Stress is a constant companion in life—whether it's money, work, or family, it seems like there's always something adding pressure. For many, it can feel like carrying a heavy rock on their shoulders, weighing them down. The truth is that stress happens when **pressure exceeds capacity**—just like a bridge buckling under too much weight or a chair breaking under pressure. The bad news? The pressure will never fully go away. The good news? We can **increase our capacity** to handle it.

We can manage stress without breaking under its weight when we intentionally build resilience. Rest, self-awareness, community, and faith all play a crucial role in strengthening our ability to withstand life's challenges.

THE KEY TO HANDLING STRESS IS INCREASING YOUR CAPACITY

We can't always control the pressure, but we **can** expand our ability to handle it. The stronger we become mentally, physically, and spiritually, the less likely we are to break under life's weight.

I encourage you today to identify which area of your life needs the most strengthening:

1) Rest and recovery
2) Knowing your identity and self-worth
3) Clarifying your purpose
4) Surrounding yourself with the right people
5) Leaning on faith

I encourage you today to choose one area and dedicate fifteen minutes a day to strengthening it. Small, consistent efforts lead to a greater capacity for handling stress.

VERSE:

"Come to me, all you who are weary and burdened, and I will give you rest."
(Matthew 11:28)

DAY 34

BECOMING THE YOU OF YOUR INDUSTRY

I became obsessed with the story of Jesse Cole the minute that I read his book, *Find Your Yellow Tux*! I even ordered and wore a yellow tux to my all-team leadership retreat one year and made his book the theme for that year! In a world where businesses often compete by following the same worn-out strategies, Jesse Cole did something different. He didn't just start another baseball team—he created a *movement*.

Starting with an underperforming team in a near-empty stadium, Jesse and his wife, Emily, were soon drowning in debt. Traditional marketing wasn't working. The fans weren't showing up. Everything seemed to be failing—until they decided to stop blending in and *start standing out*.

They didn't try to be the best baseball team. They tried to have the most *fun*.

From a dance team of senior citizens (the "Banana Nanas") to players wearing green uniforms before they had even fully branded themselves, everything about the "Savannah Bananas" was built around *fans first, entertainment always*.

Today, the Savannah Bananas sell out every game, with a waitlist of over 12,000 people. Their brand is unforgettable because they stopped chasing conventional success and started creating *moments that fans would never forget.*[6]

The biggest secret to success that I learned from Jesse? *Stop competing and start creating!*

Your industry might be flooded with competition, but **no one can compete with what only you can offer.** The businesses that thrive aren't the ones that try to be better than everyone else. They're the ones that make others want to be like them.

I encourage you today:

- » Identify what makes you **truly different**—not just better, but unique.
- » Ask yourself: What experience do I create that no one else does?
- » Brainstorm one way to make your clients feel like **raving fans**, not just customers.

VERSE:

"Do not conform to the pattern of this world, but be transformed by the renewing of your mind."
(Romans 12:2)

---

[6] Jesse Cole, *Find Your Yellow Tux: How to Be Successful by Standing Out* (New York: Lioncrest Publishing, December 22, 2017).

DAY 35

NEVER SPLIT THE DIFFERENCE: THE POWER OF NEGOTIATION

Coming from nearly two decades in the real estate industry and leadership, negotiating is something I have learned is a mastered skill that can have tremendous rewards when done the right way. Chris Voss spent years negotiating in the highest-stakes situations imaginable—hostage crises where lives hung in the balance. But his biggest lesson? **Never split the difference.** He learned that meeting in the middle often leads to resentment, dissatisfaction, and missed opportunities. Instead, the key to winning negotiations is emotional intelligence, strategic silence, and truly understanding the other person's emotions and motivations.

Whether in a life-or-death scenario or a high-stakes business deal, Chris found that the person who stays calm, listens deeply, and controls the conversation—not through aggression but through empathy—wins.

Why meeting in the middle doesn't work: In business and life, we often compromise too quickly. We're taught to "meet in the middle," thinking it's the fastest way to resolve conflict.

But here's the truth:

- » Every time you split the difference, you feel like you gave more than the other person.
- » People don't remember fairness; they remember how they felt.
- » The best deals happen when both sides feel understood, not when they reluctantly agree.

Chris didn't persuade terrorists by offering them "fair" deals. He led them to conclusions through carefully crafted questions, silence, and a deep understanding of human nature.

I encourage you today to think about this: The next time you're negotiating—whether it's for a business deal, a home sale, or even with your kids—**pause for three full seconds before responding.** Instead of trying to find the middle ground, ask: "How am I supposed to do that?" and let the other person work toward a solution. Practice getting a "that's right" response from someone. Summarize their feelings so well that they feel truly heard and understood.

VERSE:

"The heart of the wise makes his speech judicious and adds persuasiveness to his lips."
(Proverbs 16:23, ESV)

DAY 36

BECOMING YOUR FUTURE SELF

At seventeen years old, YouTube sensation Mr. Beast recorded videos speaking directly to his future self, setting bold goals with unwavering belief. He didn't just hope—he spoke as if it was already happening.

The result? He went from 8,000 subscribers to over 40 million in just five years, becoming one of the fastest-growing YouTubers in history. His story is a testament to a powerful truth: **Your future is not dictated by your past—it is pulled forward by your vision.**

Most people set goals based on *where they've been* rather than *where they are going.* They use their past experiences as a measuring stick for what's possible. But research shows that we don't act based on our past—we act based on the future we believe in. Your mindset, actions, and habits today are shaped by your vision of your future self. The clearer the vision, the stronger the pull toward it.

I've had the privilege of learning from Dr. Benjamin Hardy, author of *Be Your Future Self Now*, and he emphasizes that *we must live from our future, not just toward it.*[7] That means making

---

[7] Dr. Benjamin Hardy, *Be Your Future Self Now: The Science of Intentional Transformation* (Carlsbad, CA: Hay House, Inc., June 14, 2022).

decisions, taking risks, and aligning our daily actions as if our future self has already arrived. Just like Victor Frankl, who survived the Holocaust by clinging to the hope of reuniting with his family, your **purpose for the future determines your survival and success today.**

I encourage you today to write a letter or record a video for your future self—six months, one year, and five years from now. Speak as if you've already achieved your biggest goals. Identify one decision you can make today that aligns with your future self's success.

VERSE:

"Where there is no vision, the people perish."
(Proverbs 29:18, KJV)

DAY 37

THE SIX HUMAN NEEDS: UNDERSTANDING WHAT DRIVES YOU

What shapes your decisions and behaviors? This has been a fascinating exercise for me over the years, which I believe will be powerful for you also if you choose to do this today.

We all have six core human needs that drive our actions, decisions, and emotions. Understanding these needs helps us live more *intentionally* and align with our values:

1) **Certainty and Comfort:** The need to feel safe, secure, and in control.
2) **Uncertainty and Variety:** The need for excitement, adventure, and surprises.
3) **Significance:** The need to feel unique, valued, or important.
4) **Love and Connection:** The need to feel deeply connected to others.
5) **Growth:** The need for continuous learning and development.
6) **Contribution:** The need to give back and serve others.

Which of these needs drives you?

- » Rank your top three in order of importance.
- » Why is your #1 need the most important to you?
- » How does this need show up in your decisions and daily life?

True fulfillment comes from growing and giving. When you commit to personal development and helping others, your life gains more meaning.

I encourage you today to journal on your top need. Why is it important? How does it shape your life? Look for opportunities to grow and contribute daily.

VERSE:

"Each of you should use whatever gift you have received to serve others, as faithful stewards of God's grace."
(1 Peter 4:10)

DAY 38

THE POWER OF FUTURE-FOCUSED WEALTH AND HEALTH

Building wealth and optimizing health are not just about success; they are about freedom, longevity, and impact.

David Osborn's journey began as a real estate novice, unsure of his path but willing to learn, take risks, and surround himself with high achievers. Over time, he built a real estate empire, became a leader in GoBundance (a mastermind group for male millionaires), and optimized his health through intermittent fasting, meditation, and strategic goal setting.

But it wasn't always easy. Like many, David had to navigate fear, uncertainty, and the temptation of comfort. Instead of succumbing to doubt, he committed to personal growth, leveraged relationships, and took intentional action—a formula that led him to both financial freedom and peak health. As David once remarked in a talk I attended:

> *"Success is not about what you achieve today, but about who you are becoming for the future."*

Whether it's financial independence, personal health, or career growth, the key is not just working toward goals—but living from them. The wealthiest and healthiest people don't let life happen to them; they create systems, habits, and environments that shape their future selves.

I encourage you today to identify one financial goal and one health goal that will make the biggest impact on your future self. Write a one-year, three-year, and five-year vision for both. Surround yourself with people who challenge you to grow—whether through mastermind groups, mentorship, or books.

(If you need a place to start, read *Wealth Can't Wait*,[8] *Think and Grow Rich*,[9] or *The 15 Commitments of Conscious Leadership*.[10])

VERSE:

"The plans of the diligent lead surely to abundance, but everyone who is hasty comes only to poverty."
(Proverbs 21:5, ESV)

---

[8] David Osborn and Paul Morris, *Wealth Can't Wait: Avoid the 7 Wealth Traps, Implement the 7 Business Pillars, and Complete a Life Audit Today!* (Austin, TX: Greenleaf Book Group Press, 2017).

[9] Napoleon Hill, *Think and Grow Rich* (Chicago, IL: The Ralston Society, 1937).

[10] Jim Dethmer, Diana Chapman, and Kaley Klemp, *The 15 Commitments of Conscious Leadership: A New Paradigm for Sustainable Success* (Roseville, CA: Conscious Leadership Group, 2015).

DAY 39

THE POWER OF MINDSET IN LIFE'S UNEXPECTED MOMENTS

Your mindset is the foundation of your resilience—strengthen it before life tests you.

A couple of years ago, two weeks of my life were an absolute whirlwind of challenges for me. First, I made a major career decision to step down from a regional leadership role—a tough choice that weighed heavily on my heart. After finally finding peace in my decision, I took a spontaneous trip to Tennessee for some personal time.

Then, life threw another curveball. My long-standing 293-day Bible app streak ended simply because my phone was dead. As trivial as it sounds, it deeply frustrated me—a small, personal commitment that suddenly slipped away. Then, just as I was gearing up for a big event, my husband tested positive for COVID, forcing us into quarantine.

One challenge after another. I found myself battling negativity, frustration, and doubt. It reminded me that even when you work on your mindset often, life can still shake you—but your response is what truly matters.

Ships don't sink because of the water around them; they sink because of the water that gets inside them. Don't let external negativity take root in your mind.

I encourage you today to perform a thought audit. Take stock of your daily thoughts—are they lifting you up or pulling you down? Ask yourself:

- » Are my thoughts building or tearing me down?
- » Do I worry more than I trust?
- » Am I holding onto negative thoughts that are limiting me?

Make intentional efforts to shift towards positive, empowering thinking.

VERSE:

"So do not fear, for I am with you; do not be dismayed, for I am your God. I will strengthen you and help you; I will uphold you with my righteous right hand."
(Isaiah 41:10)

DAY 40

REFRAMING YOUR MINDSET WITH THE STORY MODEL

Today I am going to share a model that my husband loves and has taught hundreds, if not thousands, of people: The Story Model. Your thoughts create your reality—so how can you rewrite the story you tell yourself?

This simple but transformational framework reveals how we instantly attach meaning to everything that happens to us—whether good or bad.

For example, have you ever received a short or vague text from someone and immediately assumed they were upset with you? Maybe you started overanalyzing the message, reacting emotionally, and before you knew it, you had created an entire story in your head about why they were mad, how they always treat you this way, and what you should do next. But what if they were just busy? What if their phone was dying? What if their message wasn't meant to sound short at all? This is how our brains work. We experience an event, react instantly, make a judgment, and then create a story. The problem? That story isn't always true—and if we don't catch it in time, it can lead to negative emotions, bad decisions, and even self-sabotage.

Your mind will always seek evidence to confirm the story you tell yourself—so make sure you're telling the right one.

Here is The Story Model to reframe your thoughts:

1) **Something happens** (12 o'clock): An event occurs.
2) **React** (2 o'clock): Your instant emotional response.
3) **Judgment** (4 o'clock): You assign meaning to the event.
4) **Story is created** (6 o'clock): You shape a belief based on your judgment.
5) **Seek evidence** (8 o'clock): Your brain looks for proof that your story is true.
6) **A new future is created** (10 o'clock): You act based on your belief, reinforcing it as reality.

I encourage you today to think about the last time this model proved to be true for you. The next time this happens, ask yourself: *Is this story true? What evidence do I have that contradicts it? How can I choose a better story that serves me?*

VERSE:

"Love bears all things, believes all things, hopes all things, and endures all things."
(1 Corinthians 13:7, ESV)

DAY 41
INTENTIONALITY AS A SUCCESS FACTOR

You can learn accidentally, or you can learn intentionally.

This sentiment has been one that sticks, and here's why: When you want to unlock personal growth, business growth, relationship growth, or really any category of growth in your life, the quickest way to do it is to LEARN and GROW in that area. In almost every situation, you have to grow your way to success. Ambition can get you in the door, but your growth as a leader or businessperson and the ability to learn with intention will keep you in the room. Many people get "replaced" because they stop intentionally growing. They stay stagnant and stale, or they drift. They refuse to learn new ways or to invest in growth as a strategy.

Are you growing randomly or intentionally?

I encourage you today to answer the question above and discover *how* you are growing. When was the last time that you put yourself in a room to grow? To get better? Showed up as the least smart person in the room to grow to your next level of success? If it's been a while, get something on your calendar. Schedule a way to intentionally learn from people who are already doing what you want to do or accomplish.

VERSE:

*"Always remember what you have been taught,
and don't let go of it. Keep all that you have learned;
it is the most important thing in life."*
(Proverbs 4:13, author paraphrase)

DAY 42

YOUR HEALTH

Okay, I know I may have lost some of you just with today's title but hang with me. I want to talk about your health. Your actual physical body, your temple, the one and only body that God gave to you while on Earth and how you are intentionally taking care of it (or not taking care of it) as a leader.

Several years ago, I could not have written today's words. I was terrible to my body. I ate badly, I drank, I didn't exercise, I even smoked cigarettes at one point in my life (gasp, I know!)—all things I regret to this day! However, one of the greatest lessons I believe we learned throughout the 2020 pandemic, and that I have personally seen over the last few years of my life, is that when you are not intentional in taking care of your temple and do not have your health, you have nothing. Nothing. It doesn't matter how much money you have, what you do for a living, or what kind of house you have. If you don't have your health—to enjoy those things or experience the freedom from worrying about it—everything else becomes secondary.

The person who has taught me the most about being intentional with my and my husband's health has been our friend, Justin Roethlingshoefer, founder of OWN IT. Justin teaches about intentionally taking ownership of your health. He teaches that your body is a tool to fulfill the calling on your life. WHOA! Read that again. Your body is a tool. A tool to fulfill your calling. That is huge. Are you treating it that way, and are you living a life by default or a life by design? Justin taught me four key data points that drive your life span:

1) **Your HRV** (heart rate variability): This is how your body adapts to stress and strain. If you own a wearable, like an Oura ring or a Whoop, you can track those markers. It is extremely eye opening.
2) **You're morning and evening routines in the "Immediate 4"**:
   > Temperature (heat in the morning and cool in the evening)
   > Light (brightness in the morning and dimness in the evening)
   > Water (twenty ounces with electrolyte first thing in the morning and 10 percent or less of your water intake after 5 p.m.)
   > Air (two quick in, one out, ten times in the morning and in for four seconds, out for eight seconds in the evening)
3) **Wake and sleep cycles optimization:** Going to bed at the same time and waking up at the same time.
4) **Nutritional and cellular testing:** Filling your body with the nutrients and supplements that you need on a cellular level for only your unique body.

Some of you are already great at this, and some of you really need to be more intentional with these things. The reality is, if we don't fight for our bodies and our health, no one else will. Earlier this year, I somehow contracted a parasite and nine bacterial infection strains in my gut. When I finally got my results back months later, my doctor forwarded the email to me. The subject read:

"Ouch." It made me laugh a little. The point is, I was so miserable for months, and I know that I wasn't performing at my best level because my health was suffering. It made me so grateful for the health I have had, and I also saw it as a wake-up call from God to focus more on being intentional with how I treat my body. We all need to.

I encourage you today to think about how you treat your body. Your health? Are you intentional, and when did you last spend time putting an intentional plan together to focus on your longevity and health? (Following Justin R. is a great start, by the way. He has taught me so much and has such a gift in this space.)

VERSE:

"Or do you not know that your body is a temple of the Holy Spirit within you, whom you have from God? You are not your own, for you were bought with a price. So glorify God in your body."
(Corinthians 6:19-20, ESV)

DAY 43

FOUR BUILDING BLOCKS OF FAITH

I once heard a pastor speaking on the building blocks of faith, and how, as a leader or businessperson, you can only go as far as your fuel will take you. But it is your faith and belief system that FUELS you as a believer. Sometimes I look back on my life and see that, many times, I thought that my own powers and strength were fueling my success. As I have gotten older, wiser, and stronger in my faith, I know that is simply not true. Four areas are the true building blocks of faith, and they can open doors that neither you nor anyone else can open. If you are intentional with implementing them, they could be your lifeline when you run up against limitations.

Building Block #1: Grow closer to God (read your Bible, pray, fast, worship)—James 4

Building Block #2: Community of other believers (go to a church, invest in godly relationships, accountability)—Hebrews 4

Building Block #3: Walk in obedience (your habits, your talents, and your treasures are what shrink the gap between who you want to be and who you really are.)—Proverbs 3

Building Block #4: Share your faith (your work as worship, seize the moment, your scars are your story)—Acts 2

I encourage you today to think about this: Whether you just did it this morning or it's been years since you have opened a Bible, use the Bible app or grab a Bible today and just open it and read one of the chapters above that most aligns with the building block you gravitated towards the most. Think about intentionally growing in those four areas and spend a minute or two journaling about where you currently are and where you want to be in each one.

VERSE:

"For we live by faith, not by sight."
(2 Corinthians 5:7, NIV)

DAY 44
LEAVING A LEGACY

I will never forget the time that I heard my mentor, John Maxwell, speak in November 2024 on his "BIG BUCKET LIST" . . . wow. It marked me for life. John shared a list of thirteen things that he still wanted to complete in his late seventies to intentionally leave the legacy that he desires to leave. These weren't just small bucket list things. I'm talking about things like influencing and adding value to 2 million people a month, writing 101 books (he had written ninety books at the time), experiencing the transformation of a country, and seeing one million people each month receive Christ, to name a few. I think we can all agree, these are BIG things.

What I loved the most about the items on this list was that they had nothing to do with John. They were all about others. This list was so big; it was BEYOND John. He could never, ever, ever complete it on his own. He would have to include others. Especially God. That is the cool thing about this concept and the intentionality behind the exercise. If you want to leave a legacy as a leader, you've got to be thinking BIG and thinking intentionally.

I encourage you today to make yourself a "big boy list" or a "big girl list"—one that makes you wake up in the morning and GULP, instead of yawn. One that will stretch you, make you pray more, and is so big that if God doesn't do it, you won't get there. What would be on your list?

VERSE:

"Now to him who is able to do immeasurably more than all we ask or imagine, according to his power that is at work within us, to him be glory in the church and in Christ Jesus throughout all generations, for ever and ever! Amen."
(Ephesians 3:20-21)

DAY 45

LEADING VS. ACCEPTING YOUR LIFE

Unfortunately, most people don't **lead** their lives; they accept their lives, and an accepted life is an unintentional life.

I don't know about you, but I want to lead my life and lead it intentionally. I know that might sound overkill to some people, yet I have seen certain people in my life—some even family members—just accept their lives the way they are. They accept the cards they were dealt or the home they were born into. Sometimes, they even accept the habits that they were taught and the thinking that was ingrained in them from a young age. An example would be someone still getting high every day, working at an entry-level minimum wage job because that is what their parents did, and choosing to hang out with people going nowhere as an adult because, again, that is what they were taught. They simply chose not to live a life on purpose; they chose to accept their life, and as sad as it is, they will reap what they have sown.

I share this not to be negative but to be real—we all know people who are accepting their lives. It may not look as extreme as my examples, but they are still accepting their lives in little ways instead of intentionally making a life for themselves, a life of abundance and exceedingly more, which is what God wants for us. It's what He created us to have and how He wants us to live. As fast as time goes these days, what do you want your next five, ten, or fifteen years to look like? How do you need to lead your life in order to make that happen?

I encourage you today to identify someone who has accepted their life. What about that person do you believe is causing them to accept versus lead? If you were to tell your child how to lead their life versus how to accept it, what would you tell them? Now, think for a moment—do you need to tell yourself that too? Or are you currently leading your life?

VERSE:

"Show me the right path, O LORD; point out the road for me to follow. Lead me by your truth and teach me, for you are the God who saves me.
All day long I put my hope in you."
(Psalm 25:4-5, NLT)

DAY 46
BECOMING A ONE PERCENTER

I once saw this image that looked like a barcode with lots of straight vertical lines side-by-side, some higher than others. Then, at the top of the image was a rectangular box around the very tip top of the lines. Only three or four of the hundreds of vertical lines reached high enough to be in this rectangular box. The image was a picture of the one percenters out there.

A "one percenter" is, by definition, an individual who demonstrates extraordinary skill, achievement, and dedication within their chosen field, standing out from the vast majority of practitioners.

Many of you reading this today are likely one percenters. You are the best of the best; you stand out among your peers. You perform and you succeed. As an entrepreneur and business owner, I am challenged daily with finding other talented individuals who are one percenters who can continue to grow my companies. One percenters are rare. My question to you today is, how intentional are you about either becoming a one percenter or staying a one percenter?

I encourage you today to write down a few traits that you believe make someone a one percenter. Why is it important for you as a leader or business owner to be a one percenter and then attract other one percenters to your world?

VERSE:

*"Whatever you do, work at it with all your heart,
as working for the Lord, not for human masters,
since you know that you will receive an inheritance from
the Lord as a reward.
It is the Lord Christ you are serving."*
(Colossians 3:23-24)

DAY 47
THE RANCH

In 2023, I was having a great year in business and life in general. Things were really firing on all cylinders, and then a "life's unexpected" happened in July 2023. My dad passed away very unexpectedly, and it rocked my world. If you've lost a parent too soon, you get it. If you haven't, you're blessed and should be grateful. It is so hard. So, so hard. A couple of months after my dad passed, I was still grieving yet received an amazing invitation—as a top fifty operator in the entire company!—to go to Austin, Texas, that November to visit Gary Keller's ranch! It was such an honor, and I couldn't wait to attend.

While at the ranch, I got to mastermind with fellow peers, learn from a great mentor, and have a little fun, which included touring the ranch on an ATV with Gary and getting to see all the beautiful wildlife that inhabited the farm. We saw a herd of oryx. They were beautiful, and when they ran across the field at sunset, I snapped a really great photo on my cell phone to show my husband. When I got home from the ranch, I looked again at the photo and decided—because it was so good—to print it, frame it, and send it to Gary as a thank you for having me. One small, yet intentional act on my part.

Fast forward to Thanksgiving a few weeks later. We always spent Thanksgiving with my dad. We loved to cook and eat and just be together. This was my first Thanksgiving without him, and I truthfully did not even want to celebrate the holiday. Oh, not to mention, I was also turning forty on Thanksgiving that year, as well. We were supposed to go to Europe that day, but canceled because I wasn't in the right headspace. So, my husband and I spent Thanksgiving in one of my favorite places, the mountains of North Carolina. Just us two.

We escaped to High Hampton, and as we were sitting in rocking chairs, taking in the beauty of the place on Thanksgiving, I looked down at my phone and an email from Gary Keller popped up! I was thinking, *Is this spam? It's Thanksgiving!* But it was not. It was a genuine email from Gary with a picture of the oryx he had taken, with a simple note:

> *Happy Thanksgiving, thankful for your life. Thank you for your kind note, Dana. Your oryx picture is framed at the ranch, so when we took this shot, I thought of you. We have so much stress in our lives right now, yet we have so much to be thankful for. I choose to be thankful and grateful, and I know you do too.*

Wow. That one short and simple email meant so much to me, especially at a time when I needed it the most. Can you imagine the founder and owner of your company of 180,000 associates sending you an email like this? It meant so much to me. And it truly all came from one little intentional action that I took to frame a picture, write a note, and stick it in the mail.

I encourage you today to come up with a way or two that you can be more intentional this week with people in your life whom you are grateful for. They may be little things like a handwritten note. If you really want to be restored in your life and business, you will find that little, intentional actions such as mine and Gary's are the big game changers!

VERSE:

*"All hard work brings a profit,
but mere talk leads only to poverty."*
(Proverbs 14:23)

DAY 48
CHILDHOOD TRAITS

Have you discovered what your gifts are? I am not talking about the things you think you are pretty good at. I am talking about the God-given gift or gifts that only you have. The ones that were breathed into you at birth, that make you who you are, the talents that God gave you to go out and multiply in the world.

Some studies show that when adults understand what their gifts are, they look back to childhood and can usually find or remember discovering those gifts or seeing them play out in their lives somewhere between the ages of eight and twelve years old.

For example, my friend Linda McKissack is a big dreamer. She is a visionary, and she is always thinking about new projects and dreaming up business ideas. She recently shared with me that when she was nine years old, she remembers dreaming all the time. She would dream up ideas and things that she wanted to do in the future and write and draw about them. This is a gift of hers. God has given her the gift of dreaming and having a big vision.

I remember a few years ago, I took our daughter, Amelia, and her best friend, George, back to Kentucky with me for a week of fun and work. They were eleven years old at the time. I threw some company logo shirts on them, and we went to visit my brokerages for a day. They were "working" and loved it. I remember watching their actions. Amelia was cleaning and organizing the offices, making sure things looked good and working on projects. George was talking to everyone, greeting and asking them questions, and building relationships with them. I could see their gifts shining. I know that they will intentionally use those gifts as they continue to grow into adulthood, and I can't wait to see what they do with them in the future. (The funniest part of the day happened on the drive back home that afternoon from "work." After only about five minutes, I turned around to see them both passed out in the back seat, exhausted from the day. Ha!)

The lesson here today is this: When you look back on your childhood and then look at your life today, no matter your age, do you see a correlation? Do you remember hearing stories about you as a child and what you liked to do, and do you recognize them as the gifts that God has given you?

I encourage you today to make a list of what you believe are your TRUE God-given gifts and write them down. Meditate on them for a minute and thank God for the gifts that He has given only to you. How are you using your gifts?

VERSE:

"All believers have received at least one spiritual gift from God, and they are not to hoard these gifts but use them faithfully as stewards of God's grace."
(1 Peter 4:10-11, author paraphrase)

DAY 49
DIVINE SURPRISES

As a leader or business owner, I am curious: Do you like surprises? Or are you one of those people who likes to know every detail and zero surprises? I am a bit of an "in the middle" type of person. Sometimes, I like surprises, but most times, I like plans. Yet when it comes to *divine surprises*, I am all on board!

Divine Surprise = The hand of God showing out in your life, unexpected favor, God's surprise!

Said another way, this is favor you can't outrun—it's breaks you didn't expect and favor that thrusts you into your destiny! Who couldn't use a little more of that? I know I sure can!

So, how do you intentionally receive more divine surprises in your life?

It's actually simpler than you probably think: *You don't have to chase the blessings or surprises. If you chase God, the blessings and surprises will chase you!*

If you keep God in first place, you won't be able to outrun them. His blessings will overtake you because you're chasing Him. He will step in and do what only He can do! When you obey what God tells you, He will bless you so much that it spills over into the people connected to you too.

God is famous for His surprising acts. In fact, the entire book of Job is about this.

God sees you! You are in position for divine favor and supernatural surprises. He sees you blessing others; He sees you going the second mile, doing the right thing, working like you are working for Him in everything you do, prioritizing Him first, and intentionally showing up when you don't feel like it. He sees you.

I encourage you today to spend some quiet time thinking about receiving divine surprises. Thank God in advance for those surprises to come, and be open to obeying and receiving them, especially in your business.

VERSE:

"If you listen obediently to the Voice of GOD, your God, and heartily obey all of his commandments that I command you today, GOD, your God, will place you on high, high above all the nations and worlds. All these blessings will come down on you and spread out beyond you because you have responded to the Voice of GOD."
(Deuteronomy 28:1-3, MSG)

DAY 50

HAVE YOU FILLED A BUCKET TODAY?

There is a children's book called *Have You Filled a Bucket Today?* by Carol McCloud.[11] The book is a guide to daily happiness for kids. I have used this book for over a decade now in the business world and with my teams. It is fabulous. While it is a children's book—and illustrated beautifully, I might add—it packs a punch when used intentionally for adults, as well.

I have been known to take this book, pull up a stool at the front of the room of our team meetings, and read the book front to back aloud to the room. The premise of the book (not to spoil it) is that every person you come in contact with is carrying around an imaginary bucket. Your spouse, your kids, your friends, your neighbors, your employees, your work peers, your boss . . . everyone. Your bucket has one purpose, and that is to hold your good thoughts and good feelings about yourself. You feel very happy and good when your bucket is full, and you can feel sad and lonely when your bucket is empty. The way it works is that you need other people to fill your bucket, and you need to fill other people's buckets too.

---

11 Carol McCloud, *Have You Filled a Bucket Today?: A Guide to Daily Happiness for Kids* (Northville, MI: Ferne Press, 2006).

So, how do you become a "bucket filler," you may ask? By intentionally showing love to someone, being kind, giving them a helping hand or smile, or doing something to make them feel special or make their day. I don't know about you, but I want to be a GREAT bucket filler. I want to fill someone's bucket every day. You will have to be intentional in making it happen until it becomes a habit. Then, at the end of each day, ask yourself one simple question: *Did I fill a bucket today?*

I encourage you today to ask yourself when you last filled someone else's bucket. What is one thing you could do today to fill someone's bucket? How can you make this a new and intentional part of your day?

VERSE:

*"A generous person will prosper;
whoever refreshes others will be refreshed."*
(Proverbs 11:25)

P. S.—This is one of my life verses!

DAY 51
THE DISEASE OF DISTRACTION

When I was a young leader, distraction was (and if I am being honest, still is today) one of my biggest hurdles to succeeding in what I wanted to accomplish. Then, I heard this one quote that changed my mindset and life:

> *"The enemy doesn't have to destroy you;*
> *he simply has to distract you."*

Whoa. That hit. When I looked closely at certain areas in my life, I was absolutely, 100 percent letting distraction pull me away from my calling. Today, we have so many distractions. Our phones and computers are at the top of the list. Today's average person only has an attention span of less than six seconds. The enemy loves to distract us from accomplishing our calling and living out the life that God has already planned in advance.

Here are a few ways that we can be distracted from our calling:

1) **Busyness over fruitfulness.** We stay in constant motion, mistake activity for progress, and miss divine direction.

2) **Overwhelm and burnout.** We are convinced that everything depends on us, so we operate outside of the rest and rhythm we need.
3) **Offense and bitterness.** Sometimes, small wounds from others distract and take us out. Unforgiveness can clog our spiritual authority and distract us in many ways.
4) **Good things over God things.** We are filled with "good" opportunities that keep us from missing the God assignments. This distraction is often disguised as a blessing.

I can't tell you how many times in my life and career that number four completely distracted me. I wasted so much time on "good things" when I could have spent time focusing on my true calling. Wow. It's painful to look back and think about. The truth is, distraction happens to all of us, so we have to be better at spotting the culprits ahead of time because *the more influence you carry, the more intentional the enemy becomes in his strategy.*

I encourage you today to take a good look at your life right now. Where are you distracted and how? Do any of the above resonate with you?

VERSE:

"Be still, and know that I am God."
(Psalm 46:10)

DAY 52
THE GOOD LIST: PART 1

One of my favorite scriptures for businesspeople is 2 Peter 1:5-8. I had read it numerous times without actually breaking its meaning down for those who truly want to add to their faith, and as a leader or business person, it is of utmost importance to intentionally add to our faith daily.

I am going to break this down into three parts to more deeply explore how to use the first three of the seven words from Peter's scripture as actionable verbs in your life:

GOODNESS: This is the first one that Peter mentions in the verses, and we know that firsts are important. Goodness is captured by these questions: What is your temperament while you wait? When things don't happen the way that you want? When uncomfortable, do you respond in light of the goodness of God? God's goodness is not dependent upon what you see in front of you; it is dependent upon the fact that *God is good all the time, and all the time, God is good.*

KNOWLEDGE: This is continuing to grow in your faith. Knowledge is not just information that you amass. It is what you can display; it is a true sign that what you know is what you do. Sometimes we don't need more Scripture; we need more *application* of Scripture.

SELF-CONTROL: I would argue that this one may be the most difficult for people. Self-control means that the Spirit of God, not your feelings, leads you. Will your environment dictate how you respond to things? Do you recognize this as a fruit of the Spirit, and is it a sign that you have a relationship with God? That is self-control.

Just because temptation is there doesn't mean that you have to give in to it. When you have an opportunity to give someone a piece of your mind, you may need to hold that back in order to keep some pieces of your mind! (Can I get an AMEN? Ha! That is a word!)

Remember, "Little leads to much," and sustained progress happens little by little, a small change that produces amazing results!

I encourage you today to reflect on these first three words and choose the one you most need to strengthen. Then, journal about that word and what it would look like for you to grow in that area. I would even take a moment to look up the definition of the word as well. Today, begin to set your mind on adding to your faith by growing in these three areas of the "good list."

VERSE:

"Make every effort to add to your faith goodness, knowledge, self-control, godliness, mutual affection, and love. For if you possess these qualities in increasing measure, they will keep you from being ineffective and unproductive in your knowledge of our Lord Jesus Christ."
(2 Peter 1:5-8, author paraphrase)

DAY 53
THE GOOD LIST: PART 2

As you read yesterday, you know that one of my favorite scriptures for businesspeople is 2 Peter 1:5-8.

Today, we'll go deeper on how to use the next three words in this scripture as actionable verbs:

PERSEVERANCE: This is a biggie! You may be familiar with Hebrews 12:1, which talks about perseverance. However, according to Peter, adding perseverance to your faith means hanging on a little longer for some things—we don't truly know how long those things will endure in our lives. It could take not one year, but two or three or four years. We have the ability to persevere because of our relationship with God. We can press forth towards the mark of the high calling because of the God that we have! We will need to strengthen the attribute of perseverance in many seasons of our lives.

GODLINESS: This one may sting for some people, so hang in there with me. The best way to describe this one is with this question: *When people see you, do you represent the God you serve?* It is as simple as that. The answer must be yes to apply it to your life and in your faith. Some of us may say that we go to church, but then a coworker catches wind of that and responds with something like, "Oh, wow! *They* go to church?" Yikes. Ouch. That doesn't feel good. It reminds me of someone I know who hangs in bars every afternoon after work, has been known to mess around behind his wife's back, and yet is at church on Sunday mornings. Don't get me wrong, I am not judging at all. I'm very glad that he is in the house of the Lord on Sundays, yet at the same time, I can't help but wonder whether people don't see Jesus when they see him and actually turn away from the church because of his lack of godliness. Everyone sins, and everyone can be forgiven and make a new life. But when you do, you have to possess godliness—a sign of a life changed by Jesus, my friends. Godliness is being like God.

MUTUAL AFFECTION: I love this one. Not because it is easy for me, but because I believe mutual affection really shows the heart of Jesus in leaders. Mutual affection is *how you treat people who can do absolutely nothing good for you.* That's it. It's your affection towards others, strangers, family members, coworkers, etc. Are you growing in this area? Are you really leaning into this attribute to add to your faith?

Remember, "Little leads to much," and sustained progress is little by little—a small change that can produce amazing results!

I encourage you today to think about the last time you did something for someone who could do nothing for you in return. You didn't need one single thing from them. You did it out of mutual affection and the kindness of your heart. You made something about them and not about you at all. If you cannot think of anything, do something TODAY and report how you feel afterwards. I bet you'll feel pretty darn good!

VERSE:

"Make every effort to add to your faith goodness, knowledge, self-control, godliness, mutual affection, and love. For if you possess these qualities in increasing measure, they will keep you from being ineffective and unproductive in your knowledge of our Lord Jesus Christ."
(2 Peter 1:5-8, author paraphrase)

DAY 54
THE GOOD LIST: PART 3

To wrap up our last two days, we have now gone over six of the seven attributes from "the good list" that we need in order to add to our faith as leaders and businessmen and women. I saved the last one—*love*—for its own special day. And as we know, love is the greatest of them all. It is the core attribute of God.

Here is what it means to layer love on top of goodness, knowledge, self-control, perseverance, godliness, and mutual affection:

LOVE: If you possess the first six qualities and then add love, you will receive an increased measure of favor, growth, and awareness in your life! You'll increase internally. To add love means that you love one another, extending it to all people—even your enemies, to whom you should demonstrate love through acts of kindness, forgiveness, and compassion. This love is not just an emotion but a deliberate choice and action. Jesus even stated that love for one another is a key indicator that someone is His disciple (John 13:35). Love is sacrificial and willing to lay down one's life for others (John 15:13).

So, you can now see how adding love on top of the other seven attributes is really the secret sauce. Now, if I am being real and honest, I know it is not easy to love everyone, every day. Trust me, there are some people in my life who are not easy to love, even on their best days. I believe this is why we have to be intentional. We have to be so deeply rooted in our faith that even the hardest-to-love people don't change who we are or our energy. Instead, we change theirs by the love that we show them, maybe even when their actions don't warrant it.

Remember, "Little leads to much," and sustained progress happens one step at a time!

I encourage you today: Who comes to mind right now as someone a little hard to love? Maybe even a lot harder to love. It could be someone in your family, someone who works with you, a neighbor, or anyone else. When you read over and meditate on the Scriptures and words above, how can you be obedient and take one step today to show them love?

VERSE:

"Make every effort to add to your faith goodness, knowledge, self-control, godliness, mutual affection, and **love***. For if you possess these qualities in increasing measure, they will keep you from being ineffective and unproductive in your knowledge of our Lord Jesus Christ."*
(2 Peter 1:5-8, author paraphrase)

DAY 55
THE LAW OF INTENTIONALITY

One lesson I learned early on from my mentor, John Maxwell, is the Law of Intentionality. It is so great. The entire law is about how growth doesn't just happen. Growth isn't automatic. You have to go out of your way to find growth opportunities. You may need to overcome any harmful beliefs that create gaps between you and your fullest potential. There are a few specific gaps that John teaches that I'd like to share with you today:

» **The Assumption Gap:** "I assume I will automatically grow."
» **The Knowledge Gap:** "I don't know how to grow."
» **The Timing Gap:** "It's not the right time to begin."
» **The Mistake Gap:** "I'm afraid of making mistakes."
» **The Perfection Gap:** "I have to find the best way before I start."
» **The Inspiration Gap:** "I don't feel like it."
» **The Comparison Gap:** "Others are better than I am."
» **The Expectation Gap:** "I thought it would be easier."

At different times in my life, I have experienced all these gaps, and I am going to go out on a limb and say that you have as well. I can think back to times—like when God dropped into my heart to write this book—when I was in the comparison gap . . . big time!

When I lost my dad in 2023, I really struggled with the inspiration gap for the first time in my life and didn't have the energy to grow.

No matter what season you are in today, you are likely facing one or more of these gaps, and you need to know that the only way to overcome them—and be intentional about your personal growth—is to answer two key questions:

- » Where do you want to go in life?
- » How far can you imagine going?

Then, get moving! Take action. You have to forget your motivation and just do it!

I encourage you today to spend a few minutes thinking about where you really want to go in life. Imagine the furthest you can go. What does it actually look like when you visualize it? Then, ask yourself what you need to do today to take action towards that vision.

VERSE:

"Do you not know that in a race all the runners run, but only one gets the prize?
Run in such a way as to get the prize. Everyone who competes . . . goes into strict training."
(1 Corinthians 9:24–25, NIV)

DAY 56
MOTIVATIONS

Have you ever attended a motivational speaker conference or listened to someone who people deem to be a "motivational speaker"? I used to listen to motivational speakers when I was young, and I would think, *Wow, they really came up with that! They are so smart!* Then, I realized one day that every single "motivational saying" was taken from a lesson or parable in the Bible in some way, shape, or form. ALL motivations are principles in the Bible. They're all there.

Take being organized and orderly with your work, home, car, or life. Have you ever organized something and felt so great about it? Maybe you rearranged your kitchen spice cabinet in alphabetical order, or you lined up your shoes really neatly in your closet, or you vacuumed out your car until it was spotless. Didn't you feel like you could just go out and conquer the world? I know I am not alone! Okay, do you want to know the real reason why you felt that way? It's because God is a God of "order." You were created to live in "order"—in both nature and in how you live, worship, and lead.

In the beginning, God created the heavens and the earth. He created them in an orderly and deliberate, logical sequence (Genesis 1:1-31).

> *"God is not a God of disorder but of peace."*
> —1 Corinthians 14:33

This is just one simple example of how we often miss that every motivational principle we may hear on a podcast comes from the God of the Bible.

I encourage you today to identify a biblical principle you need to study more deeply—or one where you could use a fresh spark of motivation to grow. Spend a couple of minutes thinking about this and write it down. Then, search your Bible and study that principle.

VERSE:

> *"For in Him all things were created . . . all things have been created through him and for him."*
> (Colossians 1:16)

DAY 57

SHAKE SALT AND SHINE LIGHT

For years, I had this sticker that was the outline of a salt shake and a light bulb on the back of my phone. It was a visual of Matthew 5:13-14 and was an intentional reminder of two things.

First, it was such a great conversation starter (so many people would ask me what it meant or what it was when they would see my phone), so it reminded me that as a leader, I could still share its true meaning with people in a way that would encourage them.

Second, it served as a reminder that, every day, I am to be salt and light in the business world.

Salt represents influence, preservation, and value. It makes things better!

Light represents visibility, truth, and leadership. It makes things brighter!

Have you ever had a meal that was missing just a pinch of salt? It tasted bland. It was forgettable. That is what a life without purpose feels like. We aren't called to blend in, friends. We are called to *season* the world and to *shine light* into the darkness around us.

You weren't made to dim or dilute. You were made to influence, illuminate, and invite others to experience something different.

It is a powerful call to live intentionally, stand out, and lead boldly in both faith and daily work life.

I encourage you today to ask yourself: *Where in my life am I blending in when God has called me to stand out?* Choose one way to bring light or encouragement to someone around you—intentionally.

VERSE:

"You are the salt of the Earth. . . .
You are the light of the world."
(Matthew 5:13-14)

DAY 58
EXTRAORDINARY LEADERSHIP

Let's face it, the world has plenty of ordinary leaders.

Ordinary leaders seek comfort and consensus. They are capable of getting a job done and can give direction to those they lead.

Extraordinary leaders are different. The one thing that transforms ordinary leaders into extraordinary leaders is their deliberate pursuit of making *others* extraordinary. They empower those whom they lead. They are intentional about helping others find their unique ability and then developing those talents to discover their purpose.

Ordinary leaders react to what is. Extraordinary leaders rise to what could be.

In the Bible, David wasn't just a leader. He was a leader on assignment—extraordinary in impact, even through imperfect moments.

There are a few really important strategies that I have learned from extraordinary leaders that you can use to focus on developing the people around you:

- » **Ask great questions:** Becoming a leader who listens more than you talk and asks great questions (more on this tomorrow) is a skill that will set you apart as a leader.
- » **Challenge thinking:** As an Enneagram challenger, I understand this one all too well. By challenging others, you set the stage for them to have breakthrough moments. This is huge for their clarity.
- » **Encourage a focus on solutions:** Many people that I have had the privilege of leading know that I always encourage them to have a few solutions ready when they come to me with a problem. This turns problem-bringers into problem-solvers.

I encourage you today to ask yourself: *Am I leading from comfort or from calling?* Choose one area where you've been playing it safe as a leader and take one bold step toward being an extraordinary leader today!

VERSE:

*"David had served the purpose of God
in his own generation."*
(Acts 13:36)

DAY 59

THE SECRET SAUCE: ASKING GREAT QUESTIONS

I mentioned this in yesterday's reading, but I want to expand on it a little today, as it is such an important quality of a great leader and businessperson. When you know how to ask great questions, you unlock what is quite possibly the best trait of a successful person. When you ask great questions, you get out of the people pile and help others uncover new ideas and have breakthroughs. You control the conversation—not for you, but for them—and you also show others that you care enough to listen, learn, and facilitate self-discovery.

Two people in my life are deemed "the best question askers" that I know!! They have truly mastered the art of knowing what questions to ask and when. The first is my husband. If you have ever met Adam, you know there is arguably no better question asker out there. He has no reservation or fear around asking questions (which is what makes him one of the best coaches on the planet) because he knows what powerful questions can unlock for people. The second person is my friend and mentor, Dianna Kokoszka. Dianna is *the* OG question asker, I've had the privilege to learn from her. I have traveled to many masterminds and events with Dianna, and every single time, she researches the guest speakers ahead of time and prepares questions for each of them so that she is ready if given the opportunity to ask a question. I'm not talking about two or three questions. I have seen her show up with pages of questions—between twenty and thirty questions—for just one speaker. She is prepared! She taught me to do that same thing years ago, and ever since, I have been intentional about preparing great questions.

You may be thinking, *How do you come up with a great question?* That is a great question, my friend!

Here is the answer: You do your research on them, you listen to them, and you learn about them. Then, you think about one theme or thing that you believe this person could help you with right now in your life. What would that be? And then you create a question based on that. Let's be real, with today's AI technology, you could even ask ChatGPT to generate a list of questions for you if you struggle with it.

Being prepared with great questions is the difference-maker. Don't waste the precious time that you get with people. Learn all that you can! Then, pass on the knowledge to others.

Oh, and one more key note. Did you know that Jesus was the master of questions? He asked over 300 questions in the Gospels alone! Not to gain information, but to provoke reflection, challenge hearts, and reveal truth. Jesus asked more questions than He answered—because transformation starts with reflection.

I encourage you today to write a few questions in your phone's Notes app or somewhere else so that the next time you are around someone you can learn from, you are prepared with a few great questions to ask them!

VERSE:

"Now, O Lord, give your servant a discerning heart."
(1 Kings 3:9, author paraphrase)

DAY 60
ROOTED

Have you ever closely followed someone? Maybe you've read their books, learned from them from a distance, and or even met them in real life? I have found that this can go one of two ways: You either meet them and are sorely disappointed, or you meet them, and they totally exceed your expectations—and you are so pleased!

Recently, I had the opportunity to do just that. I met someone whom I had followed and learned from afar for years, and I must say, she totally exceeded my expectations! You may follow her too. Her name is Cleere Cherry Reeves. If so, she has probably encouraged you on Instagram on Sunday evenings or Monday mornings with her wildly popular and very good "Start of the Week Encouragement."

The thing that I love the most about Cleere is how intentional she is with everything. She is intentional in staying rooted, no matter what comes her way (like her son Sledge, who was born at only one pound). Not only is she intentional in staying rooted, but she also shares how to do it with so many others.

R.O.O.T.S. is a quick lesson that I learned from Cleere that you can apply today, no matter where you are in life or business:

Rhythms: How are your daily rhythms, and do they keep you intentionally focused on what matters most?

Order: Are your priorities in order or totally out of whack?

Obedience: Do you listen and obey when you are called to do something, or do you live the life that you want to live?

Tenderness: Do you have a tender heart, even toward the difficult people in your life?

Surrender: Are you willing to surrender each day, or do you try to control every little thing?

When you study each of those words, you will find that they are instrumental in keeping your life rooted in faith. They give you that firm foundation. I promise you that this will prove to be true in your life—you will be so glad that you rooted yourself before the storm came.

I encourage you today to look at the acronym above and rate yourself on a scale of 1-5, 1 being poor and 5 being the best, on how you are practicing each of these words in order to stay rooted this year. Where do you need to intentionally improve?

VERSE:

"And the seeds that fell on the good soil represent honest, goodhearted people who hear God's word, cling to it, and patiently produce a huge harvest."
(Luke 8:15, NLT)

DAY 61
DETERMINE TO DO THE WORK

My friend, Dr. Dave Martin, writes this in his book *Creating Your Own Economy*: "The promises of God are never automatic for anyone."[12]

Prosperity is not automatic. It doesn't just happen because a person loves Jesus. We have to have work ethic—a true, godly work ethic—to receive true, sustainable prosperity. We have to nurture the type of discipline that will motivate us to work hard throughout the course of our lives. That takes intentionality and a willingness to work hard to provide for ourselves and achieve our God-given goals.

Work is a blessing! Work gives our lives purpose, and that's why we will continue to work in heaven (Revelation 22:3).

In today's culture, it seems there has been a shift from hard work to a belief that we are "owed certain things." But the Bible is clear when it says, "If anyone will not work, neither shall they eat" (2 Thessalonians 3:10, NKJV), so we have to be careful not to fall into the trap of thinking that the world owes us something because we will become dependent on others to guarantee a comfortable life.

---
[12] Dr. Dave Martin, *Creating Your Own Economy: A Guide to Financial Freedom and Generous Living* (AVAIL, 2025).

Dr. Dave Martin teaches us that this mindset will actually separate you from God's blessings.

We should have a willing attitude towards work, determined to put our very best efforts into our jobs because, after all, when it's all said and done, we aren't working for a company or person—we're really working for the Lord. So whatever role you have right now, do it to the best of your ability!

I have loved this quote for years: "Bloom where you are planted." This means that whether it's a front desk job, a cook, or a CEO, you must bloom exactly where you are planted today so that you can be promoted to the next level God has for you in the future.

I encourage you today to examine your work efforts and how you show up and invest in that work. Do you work with a great attitude and to the best of your ability, or do you suffer through the days? What is one step you can take to bloom where you are planted today?

VERSE:

"Whatever your hand finds to do, do it with all your might."
(Ecclesiastes 9:10)

DAY 62

BREAK FREE FROM A FIXED MINDSET

I used to tell lies to myself like, "I'm just not good at that" or "I could never find the time to write a book," as if my abilities were set in stone. That belief kept me stuck. In the Bible, we see the Israelites wandering for forty years, not because God's promises weren't true, but because their mindset was.

A fixed mindset says, "This is all I'll ever be."

A faith mindset says, "With God, I can become who I'm called to be."

A fixed mindset focuses on limits.

Faith focuses on growth.

A fixed mindset is stuck, fastened, and anchored, and causes you to think only limiting beliefs.

A faith mindset is a growth mindset, focused on developing, extending, maturing, stretching, and BLOOMING!

I encourage you today to identify one area where you've been saying, "I can't," and replace it with "With God's help, I can grow here." Write it down and pray over it today.

VERSE:

"For as he thinks in his heart, so is he."
(Proverbs 23:7, KJV)

DAY 63
FOCUS: PART 1

I know that I am not the only person reading this who has trouble focusing or really making the main thing, the main thing, in order to grow my businesses. We discussed distraction earlier in this book, but over the next few days, I want to lean in on four practices I have implemented throughout the years that helped me gain more *intentional focus* in my life and business—and I hope it does for you too! Let's start with the first: **The 100% Practice.**

This practice says, "You can't be 100 percent all the time, but you need to be 100 percent at the right time."

This is huge . . . so huge. I am so guilty of this. I try to be 100 percent all the time, for all the people, in all the things, and the reality is that I cannot do it, no matter how hard I try. It's not realistic. The best 100 percent wife, the best 100 percent business owner and leader, the best 100 percent bonus mom, the best 100 percent friend—to be honest with you . . . it's exhausting.

So how do you focus on being 100 percent at the right time? You prepare and plan!

As John Maxwell says, *"You have to know the moment, to meet the moment, to make the moment count."*[13]

So you focus on the plan, and you prepare. I believe it was Jack Nicklaus who said it best: "Preparation relieves the pressure." The action item for today will help you do just this!

I encourage you today to look at your calendar and ask yourself, *Where do I need to be really good today? Who do I need to give 100 percent to?* For example, you need to be 100 percent in your meeting with your top people, but you don't need to be 100 percent when you eat lunch or study.

VERSE:

"But select capable men from all people—mean who fear God, trustworthy men who hate dishonest gain—and appoint them as officials over thousands."
(Exodus 18:21)

---

[13] John C. Maxwell, quote attributed—source unspecified.

DAY 64

FOCUS: PART 2

Today, we are going to talk about the second of the four practices that will help you gain more *intentional focus* in your life and business: **The 80/20 Practice.**

You have likely heard this one before or are somewhat familiar with Pareto's principle.

This is knowing and completing your priorities to bring you the best results.

You want to know the three Rs:

1) What is **REQUIRED** of you?
2) What will give you the greatest **RETURN**? (profit)
3) What will give you the greatest **REWARD**? (joy)

Delegate the things that someone else can do—the things that you don't have to do, even if you like doing them—as soon as possible. Then, invest your time in the people with the greatest return— your top people. It can be hard, but you may need to limit some people's access to you (I am talking to myself here too) because not everyone should get your attention. You can love everyone, but they have to earn your time, and they do that by getting to the top.

I encourage you today to ask yourself: *Who is my top 20 percent? What are the big actions, people, or tasks that will give me the greatest return and reward?* List them, and then align your calendar with them.

VERSE:

"Be very careful, then, how you live—not as unwise but as wise, making the most of every opportunity."
(Ephesians 5:15-16, NIV)

DAY 65
FOCUS: PART 3

Today, we will unpack the third of the four practices that will help you gain more **intentional focus** in your life and business: **The 40% Practice.**

This was a new one for me that I've learned in the last year, and I am hopeful that you, too, will learn something new that you can apply. I learned it at a mastermind, but I believe this practice originated from Jesse Itzer. In any case, it struck me.

The practice is this: *When your mind tells you that you're exhausted, you still have 60 percent left in the tank.*

You may feel like you are done, but the truth is that you still have 60 percent left to get after it. So don't stop. Keep going. Dolly Parton, the queen herself—who is still on my bucket list too meet (anyone out there reading this have a connection? If so, remember me . . . ha!)— perfectly describes this principle: *"I never tried quitting, and I never quit trying!"*[14]

---

14 Dolly Parton, "I never tried quitting, and I never quit trying," *QuoteFancy*, https://quotefancy.com/quote/795458/Dolly-Parton-I-never-tried-quitting-and-I-never-quit-trying

When you are at 40 percent, you are not done. Persistent people spend twice the amount of time thinking not about what has to be done but about what they want to accomplish! There is a huge difference. Anticipation removes distraction!

I encourage you today to ask yourself in what area you have been feeling like you are done or exhausted, yet you know deep down that you need to keep going. Think and pray on that in silence for a few minutes today.

VERSE:

"He gives strength to the weary and increases the power of the weak."
(Isaiah 40:29)

DAY 66
FOCUS: PART 4

Today, we will discuss the final of the four practices that will help you gain more *intentional focus* in your life and business: **The 1% Practice.**

The 1% Practice may be my favorite of the four, and here is why—the top 1 percent compounds everything! You want to be a 1 percenter. The most significant and successful people I know are 1 percenters, and to be honest, they are rare today. Very rare.

If you think about it, a lot of 10 percenters are out there, yet they level off because they think they have "arrived," and then they get distracted. You can probably think of someone, and I can too, who made it pretty far up the ladder of success, but they became too comfy and distracted, which prevented them from exceeding the other 9 percenters to become a 1 percenter!

You may be asking yourself, *How close am I to the 1 percent club?* Here is a little encouragement for you to keep going: *You have to be the first to start first at whatever it is that you do.* Be the first.

I love the story of one of my mentors, Linda McKissack, who was selling real estate in Denton, Texas, many years ago. She was the very first realtor in her area to hire an assistant. The owner of her brokerage thought she was nuts. Yet Linda did it anyway, and it changed the game for her and put her right up there as the 1 percenter that she still is today! (Read more about her story in *10x Is Easier Than 2x* by Dan Sullivan and Ben Hardy.)[15] You have to start first and stay until the end.

People in the top 1 percent don't get distracted. When you leave the main thing, you don't get the main thing done.

The difference between the top 10 percent and the top 1 percent is one hundred times greater; most people stop at the top 10 percent because they get everything they need, but they lose their drive to get to the top percent

I encourage you today to think about what actually sets you apart. What is different about you than the others around you? How can you intentionally always think about what sets you apart to be a 1 percenter?

VERSE:

"Do nothing out of selfish ambition or vain conceit. Rather, in humility value others above yourself."
(Philippians 2:3)

---

15 Dan Sullivan and Dr. Benjamin Hardy, *10x Is Easier Than 2x: How World-Class Entrepreneurs Achieve More by Doing Less* (Hay House Business, 2023).

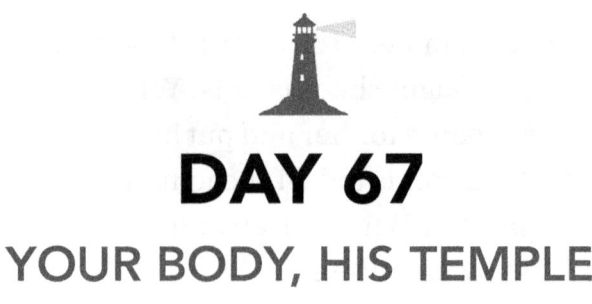

DAY 67
YOUR BODY, HIS TEMPLE

There was a season in my life when I gave everything to my goals—and I mean everything. Not proud of it, but it's the hard truth. The only thing I didn't give was my health. I stayed up late working, had horrible sleep, skipped meals, and was in constant stress. I thought discipline was just for business, until I realized: your calling requires energy, clarity, and strength! You can't pour from an empty vessel—and God never asked us to.

Taking care of your body isn't vanity—it's stewardship.

It takes intentional living to do this, and it is so worth it when you switch your mindset to live this way.

I hope you have never had a health challenge, but if you have, you know this to be true: When you don't have your health . . . nothing. else. matters. Nothing. I recently had some major stomach issues for months, and finally figured out (with the help of my wonderful functional doctor) that I had major gut infections (nine to be exact) and a parasite! Eww!

It totally threw me off my game for a few months, and I realized then just how important our health is to our lives.

I encourage you today to choose one small, intentional shift you can make for your health this week: go to bed earlier, buy an Oura ring (my favorite), hydrate more, move your body, or fuel it with REAL food, not processed. Don't do it out of pressure—do it as worship.

VERSE:

"Do you not know that your bodies are temples of the Holy Spirit. . . . Therefore honor God with your bodies."
(1 Corinthians 6:19-20)

DAY 68
OBEDIENCE OVER PERFORMANCE

I want to start today with one simple, yet powerful belief that shifted life for me: *God doesn't bless performance; He blesses obedience.*

Wow. That hit different.

For years, I thought the more I achieved, the more I would please God. I measured my own worth by results: sales, agent count at my brokerages, profit, followers, applause, etc. But burnout reminded me that God never asked me to be impressive. He asked me to be obedient. The outcome is His job. The faithfulness is mine.

God doesn't grade you on performance; He blesses you on obedience.

God doesn't reward hustle; He honors obedience.

It's not *how much* you do; it's *who* you're doing it for.

I encourage you today to ask yourself, *Am I doing this to please God or to prove something?* Then, shift your focus from, *How well am I doing?* to *Am I doing what He asked?*

VERSE:

"Obedience is better than sacrifice."
(1 Samuel 15:22, NLT)

DAY 69
BE WHERE YOUR FEET ARE

Have you ever realized that you were giving your *best* energy to everything but the people that you love most? If so, you know how painful that feeling can be. As silly as it sounds, being intentional about staying present is sometimes harder than we would like to admit.

I can think of many times when my mind has been elsewhere and I wasn't truly present with my family. I am so embarrassed to think back on it now. Nine out of ten times, it was because of my phone and the attention I was giving to someone else for our businesses who really didn't deserve it. Or it was a "fire" that needed to be put out, when, in reality, no one was dying, and it could have waited.

Presence is the most powerful gift that you can give, and it costs you everything and nothing at the same time.

I encourage you today to commit to putting your phone away during key family moments—dinner, a car ride, bedtime—just for today. Make eye contact. Ask a question. Listen on purpose. Be where your feet are.

VERSE:

"This is the day that the Lord has made; let us rejoice and be glad in it."
(Psalm 118:24, NIV)

DAY 70
BEING A SECURE LEADER

Of all the wonderful leaders that I have had the privilege of learning from, observing, spending time with, and using as models for my own leadership, one of the most important qualities that I've noticed is this: They are all secure leaders.

Secure leaders are the greatest leaders.

They aren't fighting for security, and the people that they lead can feel this.

I once knew someone who held a high role inside of a large billion dollar company, and anytime you would give him a complement or praise for a job well done, he would reply with, *"Thanks, please email that to _____"* (his boss). This was such an odd thing to me for many years, and then I realized the unfortunate truth—he was an insecure leader (unfortunate because I did like him and truly believed he did a great job).

You will need to die daily to two important things to become a secure leader:

1) The need for **approval:** "I want everyone to like me."

> Focus on the things that you are responsible for and don't worry about the rest.
> Practice selective ignorance: You don't even know they don't like you. You're just selective about what you decide to know.

2) The need for **recognition:** "I want everyone to notice me."

> Ask God, "Please don't send me out there if you're not with me."
> Visibility does not equal value. Make Jesus famous, not yourself.

I once heard Pastor Chris Hodges share a funny statement around this that stuck with me: *"Advance the kingdom and make Jesus famous over yourself because you're going to die one day, and they're gonna bury you and then eat potato salad, laugh and go down memory lane, and then go on about their lives."* :)

While funny, it is very true.

I encourage you today to lead from identity, not insecurity. Instead of striving to prove yourself, ask, *How can I empower someone else today without needing credit?* Choose to elevate, celebrate, or delegate to someone around you—even if no one notices.

VERSE:

"For we are God's masterpiece. He has created us anew in Christ Jesus, so we can do the good things He planned for us long ago."
(Ephesians 2:10, NLT)

DAY 71
BUILDING

Something funny happened to me this morning that I thought was fitting to share today. I woke up early to deeply focus on finishing this book. I went back through some old notebooks, searching for only the best lessons and stories I've learned about intentionality that I could share with you and found one from January 23, 2025. The lesson was on building and included really great prayer prompts and questions.

I read through them to decide which ones to share in this book and came across this one:

Question Prayer Prompt: "What is God calling you to BUILD this year?"

My answer:

> *God is calling me to build my book, yet the enemy is distracting me from it and I need to focus and build it to be obedient to the Lord. God is calling me to continue to build my family up in their faith. God is calling me to use my influence inside of Keller Williams for His purpose and glory. God is calling me to speak and inspire more and help change people's lives. All of this will require deep building.*

Wow. Okay, now let me share with you what is happening today, July 24, 2025, as I type this:

- » I wrote this book, and you are reading it. I'm praying that it will hugely impact on hundreds of thousands of lives.
- » Our kids just got back from church camp yesterday, where they deepened their faith. My husband and my "bonus son" are getting baptized this Sunday!
- » I had two Zooms this month with Keller Williams International about building a KW Faith Community for people of faith inside our company to join and grow in business and faith together.
- » I have had many speaking opportunities, and maybe the best one yet happened yesterday. I received an email from the assistant of one of my greatest mentors and women I admire most, Mo Anderson, asking me to speak at her regional event in March 2026. Wow. What an honor.

It brings tears to my eyes to even type this because I really see what God has built through me this year in just seven months. Yet, it truly is not about me—not at all—and it surely didn't just happen in seven months. It has happened from years of prayer and building and walking in obedience with intentionality. Wow, thank you, Lord.

You may need a reminder today to build something in the land that God has given you. When you build something that honors God, God will honor you. Keep building, friends.

I encourage you today to ask yourself the question, *What is God calling me to build this year?* and really sit in silence. Then, write down what comes to mind. The power of writing things down (look at what my writing above produced . . . mind-blowing, really—only God!) is so huge. What is God calling you to build?

VERSE:

*"Unless the Lord builds the house,
the builders labor in vain."*
(Psalm 127:1, author paraphrase)

DAY 72
BUILDERS

Yesterday we talked about building . . . and building to honor God.

Today, I want to share a few builders from the Bible with you to get your wheels turning—or keep them turning—from yesterday (known as layered learning) because I believe this will encourage many of you along your building journey.

So, who in the Bible built things?

- » **Moses:** Built the tabernacle, which God filled with His glory.
- » **Solomon:** Built the temple according to plans given to him by his father, David.
- » **Nehemiah:** Led the Israelites in rebuilding the wall around Jerusalem after their exile.
- » **Bezalel and Oholiab:** Skilled workers who helped construct the sanctuary.
- » **The builders of Shechem:** Built the field where Jacob put up his tents.
- » **The builders of Dibon, Ataroth, and Aroer:** The children of God who built these cities.

» **The builder of the Temple:** The skilled workers who cut and prepared the timber and stone.

These are just a few of the builders, but they are important to note because their roles and every single thing that they built significantly impacted a whole nation. They each had intentionality. Take Nehemiah, for example. Many things distracted him, yet he intentionally focused on his deep work of building the wall, so much so that he told the people multiple times: "I am doing a great work, and I will not come down."

All builders have these primary qualities in common:

» They do not fall to distraction.
» They are intentional with their plans.
» They build great teams around them.
» They build something that the people can look at and say, "Only God."

I encourage you today to think about what God whispered to you yesterday in your time about building. What quality do you need to possess build and finish the job?

VERSE:

"Therefore everyone who hears these words of mine and puts them into practice is like a wise man who built his house on the rock."
(Matthew 7:24)

DAY 73
WHOSE JOB IS IT?

I once heard a parable called "Who's job is it?" You may know it as the "Everybody, Somebody, Anybody, and Nobody" story. It is a widely shared story often used in leadership, teamwork, and accountability talks. I want to share it with you today:

> *There was an important job to be done,*
> *and Everybody was sure that Somebody would do it.*
> *Anybody could have done it,*
> *but Nobody did it.*
>
> *Somebody got angry about that,*
> *because it was Everybody's job.*
> *Everybody thought Anybody could do it,*
> *but Nobody realized that Everybody wouldn't do it.*
>
> *It ended up that Everybody blamed Somebody*
> *when Nobody did what Anybody could have done.*

Isn't that great? If you lead a team, or have ever led a team, then I know you laughed a little when you read that short little parable because it holds a massive truth. Here's the moral of the story: When responsibility is not clearly owned, it's easily abandoned.

Accountability turns good intentions into action. We need more intentionality in our lives around accountability.

I encourage you today to identify one responsibility you have been avoiding or assuming someone else will handle? Then, do it yourself—as worship, not obligation.

VERSE:

"Do your best to present yourself to God as one approved, a worker who does not need to be ashamed."
(2 Timothy 2:15, NIV)

DAY 74

THREE LEADERSHIP MINDSETS: PART 1

When I think of leadership experts, Craig Groeschel is always at the top of my list—someone I have learned so much from over the past two decades. He is a true expert on leadership. He teaches three leadership mindsets that have greatly impacted my life, and I want to expand on them a little today.

In order to grow faster and change more lives, you must adopt three ways of thinking. We'll start with the first.

WAY OF THINKING #1: TO GO UP, YOU MUST LET GO

I believe most leaders, including myself, struggle with letting go and leveraging the things that you need to leverage in order to succeed and achieve more. You have to do less, and you have to let go.

Think of it this way—this is such a great analogy:

Have you ever climbed a rope? My husband recently went on a "guy's trip" to the Midwest, where they did a lot of cool "guy things" like learning to pick locks, shoot firearms, and do hand-to-hand combat exercises. They also climbed a rope during a relay race challenge. Some people climbed up and touched the top with no problem (Kudos to my hubby, he was one of them!), some could get about halfway, while others could barely get their feet off the ground. The ones who made it to the top had to **let go** of the rope with one hand to reach higher and grab the rope again. Time and time again. They would have a grip, let go of the rope, and grip a higher spot. **They literally had to let go if they wanted to reach the top.** The same is true in leadership.

I encourage you today to ask yourself these questions:

1) What things can ONLY I do? (then you can determine what you need to let go of)
2) What things have I been holding onto that I can let go of, and how can I intentionally pass those off to someone else or create a system where they take care of themselves? (name them)

Then, begin to do regular audits—weekly and monthly—to help you delegate these things to those around you.

VERSE:

"You and these people who come to you will only wear yourselves out. The work is too heavy for you; you cannot handle it alone."
(Exodus 18:18)

DAY 75

THREE LEADERSHIP MINDSETS: PART 2

As you learned yesterday, three leadership mindsets teach us to grow faster and change more lives, and we covered the first one: letting go in order to go up. Today, we will cover the second one.

WAY OF THINKING #2: TO LEAD BROADER, YOU NEED TO THINK HIGHER

This one is a biggie, and I am going to give you three questions that have been game changers for me as a leader and entrepreneur. Thinking HIGHER means making time to think and work ON your business, not just IN your business. You have to disrupt your flow. Work from a different place. For me, every single time I get on an airplane, I think differently and get huge ideas (probably because there aren't any distractions)! Sometimes we have problems we can't solve because we are too close to them, so we aren't getting above them. You have to create a little emotional distance to think higher. Here are three great questions that can help you create some emotional distance in order to intentionally think higher:

1) If a great leader replaced me, what would they do?
2) If no one's feelings got hurt, what would I do?
3) If I were advising someone else in the same situation, what would I tell them to do?

All of these create emotional distance and objectivity. If you are too close to any situation, you are losing effectiveness! Force yourself to think higher and create objectives.

I encourage you today to think about a situation in your life or business right now where you need to create emotional distance in order to think higher. How would you answer those three questions in that situation?

VERSE:

"Do not be anxious about anything, but in every situation, present your requests to God. And the peace of God, which transcends all understanding, will guard your hearts and your minds in Christ Jesus."
(Philippians 4:6-7)

DAY 76

THREE LEADERSHIP MINDSETS: PART 3

As you learned yesterday, three leadership mindsets teach us to grow faster and change more lives, and we covered the first two. Today, we will cover the third and final mindset.

WAY OF THINKING #3: TO REACH MORE, YOU NEED TO KNOW LESS AND EMPOWER MORE

Your importance isn't determined by what you know but by who you empower. Empower more people to do and call what they are supposed to do, and you will reach more in return!

Craig Groeschel teaches that sometimes you have to be present, but more often than not, you need to be strategically absent. That's where the potential is. I could write an entire book on how many times I have royally screwed this up. So many times. Craig shares how he and his team appoint a campus pastor for each new church campus they launch. Then, he and his wife, Amy, visit the church on launch day, but instead of teaching or preaching on stage, they hang out in the lobby, greet people, fellowship, and just love on everyone. This is strategic because if he got on stage to teach, he would (unintentionally) steal the show and undermine the campus pastor. That would not be good because Craig won't be there the next week, or the next, but the campus pastor will.

So many times, I have hired a leader, swept into town, and then jumped up to the front of the room—not intentionally, but because I felt that's what I had to do. The truth is, sometimes we need to tolerate things outside of our preferences and embrace more flexibility so that we can empower those around us and those we lead. We need to let them lead!

Hold on tightly if you want to keep what you have, but if you want something more, let go.

Leaders have gears inside of them that have an extraordinary ability to empower and impact more people, but you have to bring out more in them. Help them pull out what God put inside of them and help them use the talents that He gave them.

You will be disappointed with what you can do in the short term, but you will be drastically amazed at what God can do in a lifetime!

I encourage you today to ask yourself, *Where do I need to be a little more strategically absent in order to empower those around me?* It may even be with your children! Think about how you could be more flexible to empower that person so that they learn on their own, and in return—you'll grow too!

VERSE:

"Humble yourselves before the Lord, and he will lift you up."
(James 4:10)

DAY 77

POSSESSING PASSION

I am going to start today by sharing one of my favorite stories about my mentor, John Maxwell, that I have ever heard him tell. The story goes like this:

John, who, decades ago, was the preacher of a very small church in a small Ohio town, had such a tremendous passion for his church and the people. He knew that God put him there to grow the church, so he set a goal for one Sunday in the future (a specific date) to have 300 people in the congregation that day, or he wouldn't preach. Everyone knew the goal, and then when Sunday finally came, the church was packed! John just knew they would hit their goal. As the people were being counted before John went up to preach, he got word of the number—298 people. He was TWO PEOPLE short of the goal. Everyone knew the deal, and he really wanted to preach that day. So John, in all of passion, got up and walked straight down the aisle, pushed open the church doors, and walked outside across the street to a gas station. There was one car there, with a man and a woman in it. John walked over to them and asked them one question, "Which one of you wants to be a hero today?"

If you know John, you probably know how the story ended. The couple walked back across the street, into the church, and sat down to be the 300th, and John walked up to the pulpit and preached.

This is a story about the power of passion.

Passion will take away all your common sense. You're caught up in what could be instead of what is because passion doesn't wait. If you have passion, you will pass most people because most people don't have any passion.

When you're dead, you lose your passion. There are a lot of alive dead people walking around.

But a person with passion will always keep beating the odds!

I encourage you today to ask yourself: *What am I truly passionate about?* If you aren't excited about what you're doing right now, what is it going to take to get you excited? If you're more excited about what you did yesterday than today, you're in trouble! So, get to dreaming!

VERSE:

"If any of you lack wisdom, you should ask God, who gives generously to all without finding fault, and it will be given to you."
(James 1:5)

DAY 78
DEEP WORK

I recently learned about the practice of *deep work* and can't believe that in all my decades of experience, I had never heard that term before.

You learn something new every day, right?

The premise of Cal Newport's book *Deep Work* is profound. He frames deep work as focused, undistracted effort that leads to excellence and legacy.[16] We've talked about distraction a lot because in order to live a big, intentional life, you have to rid yourself of distractions. You have to realize that *God does not bless busy hands—he blesses faithful ones.*

Shallow work keeps you distracted.

Deep work brings you into alignment with your purpose.

I encourage you today to block out one hour this week for uninterrupted, purpose-driven work—phone off, notifications silenced,

---

[16] Cal Newport, *Deep Work: Rules for Focused Success in a Distracted World* (New York, NY: Grand Central Publishing, 2016).

heart open. Ask God to meet you there. Focus not just for productivity but for *impact*.

VERSE:

"Make it your ambition to lead a quiet life; you should mind your own business and work with your hands, just as we told you."
(1 Thessalonians 4:11, author paraphrase)

DAY 79

VISION FIRST, THEN VICTORY

I have learned it the hard way—if you don't set the vision, others will set it for you. We sometimes chase every good idea, every opportunity, every "yes." But eventually we step back and realize that God didn't call us to do everything—He called us to do what matters most. Our calling.

Vision isn't just a leadership tool—it's a spiritual compass!

Without vision, your potential drifts.

With vision, your life aligns with divine purpose.

In 2020, my husband and I decided that we needed a vision for our family. We went through a set of exercises—including the Maxwell Values Cards—where each family member chose their top five personal values. Then, we identified the overlapping values that became a set of shared family values! I highly recommend doing this with your family and team, if you have one. After we did this, we established our family's vision, and we still have it framed in our house today:

Roach Family Vision Statement: *To become a family that is deeply rooted in faith, love, trust, and communication. We will accomplish this by consistently living by and being 100 percent committed to our family values.*

Roach Family Values:

1) **Faith** (all of us): Have faith, love, and gratitude for God.
2) **Kindness** (Amelia): Treat others as you would like to be treated.
3) **Commitment** (Addison): Be 100 percent devoted to all your commitments and see them through.
4) **Generosity** (Dana): Give daily.
5) **Fun** (Adam): Have more fun today than you did yesterday!

I encourage you today to take fifteen minutes of quiet time to pray and write down your vision—just one clear sentence for your life, business, or family. What do you want it to look like five years from now? Then, reverse engineer your steps.

VERSE:

"Commit to the Lord whatever you do, and he will establish your plans."
(Proverbs 16:3, NIV)

DAY 80

ENTREPRENEURIAL KINGDOM WORK

There was a season in my business where I was building hard but not building holy. I was chasing growth, hitting goals, and checking every strategy box, but something still felt off. That is when I had someone close to me say *"You're not just building a business. You're building a kingdom whether you realize it or not."* I began to see my business not just as a job, but as a **God-assignment.** Every offer, meeting, contract, and client became a thing or person to serve with a purpose and a chance to reflect the excellence God had put in me.

You're not just an entrepreneur, leader, or businessperson; you're an architect of impact!

When your business is rooted in obedience and built with excellence, it becomes a vehicle for eternal influence.

I have a dear friend named Gabby Maddox Davis. She is a Black business owner right in the heart of Atlanta, Georgia, and she is SO GOOD. She has built an incredible business in a short amount of time and portrays excellence and obedience in everything she does. She sees what she does as a God assignment. In the secular space, she even has her eighty-year-old grandmother lead a Zoom on faith every Wednesday morning for her businesspeople who want to participate! It's amazing to watch. Gabby exemplifies being a kingdom-builder in a secular world. She doesn't have to deliver a sermon on Sunday mornings to make a huge impact on the business world or businesspeople. She is just one example of a leader who doesn't just build the business but the kingdom too.

I encourage you today to audit your business through a kingdom lens. Ask yourself: *Where am I building out of fear or striving, and where am I building with faith?* Then, choose one area—maybe your people, pricing, process, or marketing—and bring it under God's leadership. Pray over it. Commit it. Refine it with excellence.

VERSE:

"Do you see someone skilled in their work? They will serve before kings; they will not serve before officials of low rank."
(Proverbs 22:29)

DAY 81

LESSONS FROM WINSTON CHURCHILL

In 2019, my husband and I went on the trip of a lifetime to London, England, with John Maxwell for his Equip Foundation. We did so many memorable things that the average person would never get to do. When you take a trip with John Maxwell, you get to do things that the general public does not. It's unreal. One of my favorite memories from the trip was entering a private bunker that is closed off to the public at Churchill War Rooms. Then, Churchill's grandson spoke to our group about his grandfather. It was such a learning experience.

A few facts about Winston Churchill. On September 11, 1940, Churchill had just become the prime minister and six years later gave his famous speech that was heard around the world in the basement room. He was the most human human—he loved animals! His grandson told us a story about how he loved animals so much that he couldn't carve the turkey on Thanksgiving. One day, he handed the knife to his friend and said, "You do it; he was my friend." He had a slight lisp, and he actually taught himself how to speak without it by reading books out loud while looking in the mirror.

He lived to the age of ninety and passed away in 1965. A wonderful quote hung above the flag over his coffin at his funeral that said,

"We owe you what every man, woman, and child in this country owes, liberty itself."

I learned several lessons that have helped me to lead better and also stay encouraged to lead in hard times.

- » The two words his family and closest friends most used to describe Churchill were FAITHFULNESS and DETERMINATION. It would be quite the accomplishment to be remembered by these two words.
- » A real leader always has the capacity for work. He worked very hard, and he did not give up. He was not a quitter.
- » The people loved Churchill because he always told the truth.
- » Churchill was successful because he could strategize and solve problems, took people with him and elevated them, and was so humble. He truly cared about the people. He was a man who took action when he needed to.

I could share so many great lessons from this time at the bunker in London. It's a memory that I will have forever. It taught me that our backgrounds and circumstances are what make us who we are today.

I encourage you today to think about what stands out to you the most about his leadership that you could grow in at this point in your life?

VERSE:

"But as for you, be strong and do not give up,
for your work will be rewarded."
(2 Chronicles 15:7)

DAY 82

ADVICE FOR YOUNGER GENERATIONS

I believe that there is such a calling on the younger generation right now. They are so smart and resilient, having endured wild and crazy things like a global pandemic, years of remote schooling, and learning how to navigate life online. I don't know that I could have endured all of that as a pre-teen or teen. When I think about the next generation, I think of Addison and Amelia. I am so proud of them. If you are a bonus parent, you know the role is unique and hard and joyful all at the same time. I am so blessed to get to co-parent and be a role model for them. I am just so proud of them!

I would tell the next generation four big things about being intentional in life as they grow into adulthood:

1) **Build a relationship with God.** Make Him your firm foundation. When you go through many trials (and you will), you will wade the waters very differently if you have a deep faith. You will go through life with the "God Advantage," and there is nothing else out there like it.

2) **Be yourself.** Don't be something you're not. Be authentic to yourself and learn how to connect with people in a real and authentic way.
3) **Take part in the "old-fashioned" ways of doing things when you can.** It's so great to reference, remember, and learn from tried-and-true methods. Don't rush through life.
4) **Don't be discouraged by setbacks.** Every single one of us has setbacks. You have to learn to press on!

I encourage you today to ask yourself which of the four tips above you need to really focus on in your life today. If you are not of the younger generation, take a picture of this page and send it to someone who is today. Who could use the encouragement? Maybe it's your child, nephew, employee, or neighbor—everyone needs encouragement. If you are a younger generation reading this, I am so proud of you!

VERSE:

"We will not hide them from their descendants;
we will tell the next generation the praiseworthy deeds of
the LORD, his power, and the wonders he has done."
(Psalm 78:4)

DAY 83

THE MONEY HABIT OF GENEROSITY

Whether you have a lot of money, a little money, or no money at all, intentional habits—when practiced—will pay big dividends in your life. One is the habit of generosity. You must understand the law of generosity and money habits, especially if you are a leader, and practice it intentionally.

Money gives you options. It gives you the power to choose. It also helps other people if it's used correctly.

There are two types of money: planned money and surprise money. Your tithe and other places where you know your money is going are planned money. Surprise money is the leftover with no plan attached to it—what you could spend, save, or even give away to grow in generosity.

We should all get creative with how we give our money. If you don't believe that you have money to give, I have a harsh reality check for you—you do. You are either wearing it, driving it, or eating it (funny yet very true).

Making money is a 1; giving money is a 10!

It feels so good to give to other people; in fact, I once heard someone say, *"Do your giving while you're living so you know where it's going."* SO good.

We should astound others with our generosity.

One of my life's missions is that one day, when I am gone from earth, those who know me will say "She was the most generous person and intentional gift-giver that I knew, and she gave generously no matter what!"

I encourage you today to search your heart and spend a few minutes thinking about how you can improve on the generosity habit— or maybe even just start today by being a little more generous. Take the step of intentional faith and give. You can start small. Remember, giving shows a person's heart.

VERSE:

"Give, and it will be given to you."
(Luke 6:38)

DAY 84

LESSONS FROM THE GREAT JOHN WESLEY

John Wesley is someone whom I have loved to study over the last decade. You may have heard of him. He started the Methodist Church and is known around the world for his wisdom and impact on the Methodist Church and faith world in general. While John Wesley has outlined several invaluable leadership lessons over his lifetime, I want to give you just ten short lessons today that I believe will help any leader out there—because we are all leaders, and all leaders need to get better every day!

1) Lead with **purpose**. Do it intentionally. With purpose. Not haphazardly.
2) Lead with **urgency**. This is passion! Do you have passion?
3) Lead with **hope**. Be a hope dealer. Everyone needs one.
4) Lead with **kindness**. Keep your thoughts to yourself until you can sit down and talk with that person.
5) Lead with **responsibility**. You are responsible for people. Don't even let people who are hard to have conversations with into your life. Get rid of them and surround yourself with the right people.

6) Lead with **humility**. This is the greatest quality in a human. C. S. Lewis is often attributed with having said, "Humility is not thinking less of yourself; it's thinking of yourself less."
7) Lead with **boldness**. Don't be afraid; take action.
8) Lead with **consistency**. Be punctual. Personal disciplines show up in public lives.
9) Lead with **accountability**. Have regular meetings and time with your people.
10) Lead with **purpose**. Have an organization that keeps the mission after you're gone.

I encourage you today to look at this list, decide what you need to improve, and jot down how you plan to do this with intention today.

VERSE:

"The beginning of wisdom is this: Get wisdom. Though it costs all you have, get understanding."
(Proverbs 4:7)

DAY 85
ALWAYS EXCEED EXPECTATIONS

I love to do something for someone that totally exceeds their expectations. Many mentors have taught me and modeled this over the last several years. You should intentionally look for ways to exceed expectations—especially in the business world—for your clients and colleagues. Figure out what their expectation is, make that the *floor,* and then exceed it!

The quickest way to set yourself apart from others is to exceed expectations! Today, only 15 percent of people in the marketplace actually *meet* expectations. That is sad! It's also a really sad thing when you have to ask yourself, *How do I motivate my people?* They should motivate themselves! Read that again if you are a leader with an unmotivated team. You will never win if you have unmotivated people. Okay, back to expectations.

Don't just fulfill; ask . . . and then do more!

Do MORE than people expect from you! Always.

To go above and beyond, however, you have to always intentionally get better. You have to keep improving and investing in yourself.

When you do this, you have the passion, the capacity, and the "why" to wake up every day and exceed someone's expectations.

I encourage you today to answer this question: When was the last time that someone exceeded YOUR expectations? What was it? What did it feel like? How did it set them apart in your mind? Now, how can you exceed someone's expectations today?

VERSE:

"If anyone forces you to go one mile,
go with them for two miles."
(Matthew 5:41)

DAY 86
CONSISTENCY IN LEADERSHIP

Okay, let's be honest with each other today, would you call yourself a *consistent* person by nature?

The best leaders work hard to intentionally stay consistent. My coach, Terrie Foster Nowland, has really taught me a lot about this. The thing about consistency is that if you say you're going to do something, you do it. If you say you're going to be somewhere, you're there. If you initiate a new business project or initiative, you follow through. Consistency really is a MUST as you build and grow your business.

Here's why:

1) Consistency allows for **measurement**. Until you try something for an extended period of time with consistency, you won't know if it works or not. Terrie taught me to give anything new six consistent months before judging it as a success or a failure. It's often minor tweaking instead of huge overhauls that make the difference.
2) Consistency creates **accountability**. You may expect accountability in metrics and deliverables from the people you lead, but they expect the same from your leadership in return.

Make time for your team. Do things together. Even if it's only you and one assistant or admin person.

3) Consistency establishes your **reputation**. Business growth requires a track record of success. Constantly shifting or trying new tactics can quickly become part of your reputation. Often, we see leaders initiate something significant and then abandon it or fail to follow through consistently. It's a constant "Coming Soon" or "Big Launch Coming," but you never really see it come to fruition. They'll gain a reputation for that.
4) Consistency makes you **relevant**. Your clients or team need a predictable flow of information from you.
5) Consistency maintains your **message**. Your team pays much more attention to what you do than what you say. Consistency in your leadership serves as a model for how they will behave. When something doesn't work, look back and ask yourself a serious question: Did we shift gears too quickly?

I encourage you today to think about consistency. What does it mean to you? Why is it important? How can you take one step today to improve your consistency?

VERSE:

*"Therefore . . . stand firm. Let nothing move you.
Always give yourselves fully to the work of the Lord."*
(1 Corinthians 15:58)

DAY 87
HOW TO *REAL* AND NOT WEIRD

A few big qualities come to mind when I think about the traits I most look for in the people I surround myself with, yet I come back time and time again to the most important one to me, which is **being real,** or said another way, being authentic and genuine—not fake.

You know it when you see it—someone who has everything to prove and just shows up really inauthentically. Sadly, there are some people out there who just do not know how to be real or authentic. I am sad for them. Today I want to talk about strategies for being intentionally real—without being weird.

First, too much transparency is a thing. There is a difference between being truthful to be real and being too transparent. Telling the truth means that what you say is true. It doesn't mean everything true needs to be said.

Second, you have to be self-aware. People are drawn to your authenticity, not your performance. God doesn't need you to be perfect—just present, honest, and available. You have to be self-aware about whether you are putting on a show or operating out of who you naturally are. I used to have a coworker who really was a nice person and, I believe, very talented! Yet, he could not attract people to his business or keep them because people felt he was constantly "putting on a show" and wasn't being real. That is a fixable trait, yet it takes real intentionality.

I encourage you today to think about how you can be more real with the people around you. Have you been showing up a little weird in a group or room? Are you giving them your true self? How can you change that today? What honest—not polished—word of encouragement could you share today without sharing everything?

VERSE:

"We refuse to practice cunning . . . [by] the open statement of the truth we would commend ourselves to everyone's conscience in the sight of God."
(2 Corinthians 4:2)

DAY 88
THE THREE MUST-DOS

Jack Welch is one the GOATS, as we would say today, of leadership. He was the OG—a business leader and the CEO of General Electric for many years. You can find some wonderful YouTube videos on his leadership lessons, yet one of Jack's lessons transformed me the most, along with the way I lead as a business owner today.

This lesson is the three musts of a leader:

1) You must tell people WHERE you are going.
2) You must tell people WHY you are going there.
3) You must tell people WHAT'S IN IT FOR THEM to get there.

Think about those three for a moment from a client's perspective. They will always want to know where your organization, team, group, or business is going, but if you don't know, you will have no idea how to get there. Then, you want to know why. What is the *why* behind it all? You can easily set a goal and share it as a leader, but if your people do not understand the why behind it, they will never rally or buy in to the vision.

It's the same way with our kids, right? We can tell them to do something or not to do something, but if we explain *why* they can't touch the hot stove—because it will burn their hand—then they'll fully understand it better. They'll "get it." Lastly—and maybe most importantly—once you get buy-in, everyone will want to know: What is in it for them? We can't be mad about that; we have to accept that as part of life for the people we lead, and more importantly, the people we steward. We have to share what is in it for them when we all win together.

This is one of the most powerful lessons I have learned over the last nineteen years of being in business and leadership. I promise you, if you can remember it and put it into practice, your business will grow and your leadership will be blessed. I am proof of it. You will be too.

I encourage you today to memorize these three "musts" by Jack Welch and internalize them deep down inside. Think about how you can put these into practice now in your life and work. When was the last time you shared where you're going or why you're going there? It may be time to do it now!

VERSE:

"And the LORD answered me: 'Write the vision; make it plain on tablets, so he may run who reads it.'"
(Habakkuk 2:2)

DAY 89
THE FOUR PICTURES OF GOD

It would be bold to assume that every single person who reads this book has a relationship with God. Maybe someone gave it to you or you know me and wanted to support me (thank you!), but you didn't really know what you were getting into. Either way, after today, you will have read eighty-eight days of leadership lessons and have hopefully gotten a glimpse into who I am, how you can develop your life, business, and leadership with intention, and what being a believer can do for your life. Now, I want to take an even bolder step and share the four pictures of God with you—a lesson that you can also share with others.

People who don't know God or maybe have some knowledge but no real relationship with Him as an eternal Father, have one of four pictures of God:

> **Way #1:** *A locked gate*—God can't be reached. He's too far away or behind some sort of locked gate that I will never be able to unlock because of who I am or what I've done.

Way #2: *A garbage can*—I am simply not good enough to know God or be loved by Him. I'm garbage. I'm not worthy because of what I have done in life. I've made too many mistakes.

Way #3: *An endless ladder*—I could never be good enough; there simply isn't enough time left. The ladder never stops because I've run out of time to right my wrongs and get into a relationship of faith with God.

Way #4: *A door with Christ knocking*—I know what I need to do; I know God is on the other side of this door just waiting, hoping, and asking me to open it and let Him into my life and heart.

No matter which visual you see when you think of God and religion, I pray that you open your ears and your heart to just listen today. I hope you know that there is nothing you could have done in your past that would possibly keep God from standing on the other side of the door and knocking. I value you and have prayed for every person who will touch this book or read its pages. Remember that every person we encounter in life is either a victim to exploit, a problem to avoid, or a person to be loved. I hope we choose the last one today.

I encourage you today to spend a few minutes journaling about what image of God you currently have. Is it one of the four above? How can you begin to change that image into one of a loving, Heavenly Father who gave up His only Son so that we could all screw up only to be forgiven, washed white as snow, and welcomed into a relationship with the Lord? Whether you pray every day or never pray, whisper a little prayer and ask God to send the Holy Spirit to move in your life today, and then watch what God does!

VERSE:

*"Look! I stand at the door and knock.
If you hear my voice and open the door, I will come in,
and we will share a meal together as friends."*
(Revelation 3:20, NLT)

DAY 90
BE A GREEN TAG PERSON

In 2018, I stumbled upon an old war story that truly changed me and made me a better leader and person. I want to share this story with you today as our ninety days of learning how to be more intentional in your leadership and life come to a close. I heard this story at a church conference years ago, and I pray that it impacts you like it did me.

> *If you've ever been to the emergency room, you've experienced the process known as TRIAGE. Triage is a French word that means "to sort out," and it refers to the system that doctors and nurses use to decide which patients are in dire need of help and who aren't.*
>
> *In the Allies War camp during World War II, the triage supervisor had the unenviable job of labeling the soldiers with one of three colored tags.*
>
> *The first was a red tag given to patients who were "hopeless." These patients would be made as comfortable as possible until they died. The second was a green tag given to the "hopeful." These patients were left alone because they would survive without immediate help. The third was a yellow tag given to the "doubtful." They were given the most meticulous*

and immediate treatment—treatments that would be the difference between life and death.

A soldier named Lou arrived at one of these makeshift hospitals. He had been hit by shrapnel, and one of his legs was completely shattered. He had also lost a lot of blood. The triage supervisor examined him and tagged him as "hopeless"—red. The nurse assigned to Lou noticed he was conscious, and she began talking to him. She soon discovered they were both from Ohio, and after getting to know his life story, she decided to do something that was against triage protocol, risking her entire medical career and reputation. She changed Lou's tag to "doubtful"—yellow.

A few hours later, Lou was given intensive care. He was transported from the front lines to a better medical facility, where his life was spared. He would spend the rest of his life balancing on one leg, but he was grateful to that nurse for giving him a second chance to live.

In closing, my parting words today are this:

We are all called to be tag changers. Take the green tag as a symbol. No matter the "level" in which you lead—maybe it's a small group, your family or household, or a team of hundreds or thousands—you are a tag changer! I believe that God is the God who brings dead tags back to life, and He has done that for so many of us. Now, we need to go out and change others' tags. I want you to be a tag changer—an intentional tag changer! You can start today!

I encourage you today to think about who in your life has given you a green tag. Who took a chance on you when you needed it? How can you become an intentional tag changer for the people around you?

VERSE:

"Suppose one of you has a hundred sheep and loses one of them. Doesn't he leave the ninety nine in the open country and go after the lost sheep until he finds it?"
(Luke 15:4)

ACCESS ADDITIONAL *RESTORE* RESOURCES AND CONNECT HERE:

ACCESS THE SUPPORTING 90-DAY MUSIC PLAYLIST, WORKBOOK MATERIALS, AND MASTERCLASS

RESTOREDEVOTIONAL.COM

CONNECT WITH DANA ON INSTAGRAM

@DANAGGENTRY

FOR MORE INFORMATION ON UPCOMING NEW BOOKS, SPEAKING ENGAGEMENTS, & MORE

www.ingramcontent.com/pod-product-compliance
Lightning Source LLC
Chambersburg PA
CBHW050525170426
43201CB00013B/2086